1973

HUMANISTIC TEACHING

STUDIES OF THE PERSON

edited by

Carl R. Rogers
William R. Coulson

HUMANISTIC TEACHING

Donald H. Clark

Herbert H. Lehman College
City University of New York

Asya L. Kadis

Late Director, Group Therapy Clinic
Postgraduate Center for Mental Health
New York City

CHARLES E. MERRILL PUBLISHING COMPANY
A Bell & Howell Company   Columbus, Ohio

International Standard Book Number: 0-675-09626-X

Library of Congress Catalog Card Number: 70 -173877

1 2 3 4 5 6 7 8 9 10 / 75 74 73 72 71

PRINTED IN THE UNITED STATES OF AMERICA

OUR PURPOSE

You know that you are a person, and you know that every student in every classroom is a person. But once you step inside the doors of most schools it is difficult to remember that each body represents a person who deserves respect. We offer this book as a helping hand to the teacher who wants to remember and respect.

In this book we introduce ourselves, describe the orientation that sets our style for dealing with human problems, talk about our group approach to classroom living, and then offer a chapter full of examples illustrating how we handle specific common problems. Finally we offer you our thoughts about where a school best fits into the human community.

The first chapter contains two letters, one from Asya and one from Don. The rest of the book is a blend of the two of us, but before getting into the formal content, we wanted to introduce ourselves to you as individuals. This is not a very large book and you can readily discover its flavor by leafing through it. In our letters we will tell you how it came to be—where the idea came from and what we hope to accomplish. Our purpose is to put a reference book in the hands of humanistic teachers.

CONTENTS

4. The School's Community   *157*

HUMANISTIC TEACHING

Letters from the Authors

LETTER FROM DON

Dear Reader:

I think it will make the reading of this book more enjoyable and more worthwhile if you have some feeling of what the people are like who wrote it. As a student reading texts, I always grabbed at the slightest piece of information about an author, even if it was something as distant as an obscure reference to "my own children . . . ." "My God! He's a father!" I would think. My mind would race ahead. "That must mean that he's married and lives somewhere that he calls home and that he has yelled in anger and kissed and played games and . . . ." I would find myself carried away on a humanistic wave of fantasy by the simplest personal reference. Now, years later, I have some better understanding of what was going on inside me.

Like many people, I think I had an unconscious fantasy that textbook authors were all dead, or that they lived inside the covers of their books. The books almost always seemed dull, and part of the reason was that they lacked the colorful flesh-and-blood humanness of a novel. There was little chance to use your senses vicariously while reading the textbook and there was little chance to get any feeling about the human being who had written the book.

One of my writing goals is to make textbooks as interesting to read as novels. For me, this book represents a step in that direction because I have been able to put much sensory (smell, hearing, taste, color, etc.) information into it and because I have been able to put much of me (and Asya) into it. My guess is that you would still rather curl up in bed with a mystery story than with this book, but I think we're on the right track.

But first about me, and then the book. I was born in July 1930, so I expect to be about forty-one years old by the time this book is

3

in your hands. I was born in a little seacoast town in New Jersey called Belmar. I was the last child and had been preceded by two brothers and two sisters. My mother had gone through fourth grade and my father through first grade. He was raised on a farm in northern New Jersey and never learned to read or write. I have been surrounded by educated people for so long now that, as I write, I stop and marvel that this is true. My father, who died in 1971, never knew how to read or write; in an age where rockets go to the moon it is hard to believe. But it is explained, in part, by his age. I am the youngest son of a youngest son, which stretches the generations through time. My father's father fought in the Civil War.

The year 1930 was a bad time to be born into a large family with little parental education. We had a hard time through the Depression and I learned what it means to be poor. (My definition of being poor is going to bed hungry because there is no money for food and no grocer who will extend more credit.) The miracle, looking back, is that the seven of us did make it through those years without starving to death. Besides the unpleasant memories, there are many pleasant ones. I can remember times when we all sat around the living room and sang together. I can remember putting on impromptu plays and skits for family entertainment. There was a feeling of needing one another, belonging together, and being ready to do whatever was necessary so that we could all survive. I am quite certain that those early years in the large family group are responsible for my professional interest in groups.

Elementary school was misery for me. I liked a few of my teachers and there were interesting things to do sometimes, but it was a bore at best. The children with whom I went to school were not happy. I am sure that this was in part due to the misery of the Depression years, which produced anxiety as well as empty stomachs for teachers and children alike. But I cannot forget that the teachers seemed to be two-dimensional figures who were sometimes mean and sometimes angry, but who appeared incapable of being entirely human.

The curriculum in elementary school makes me boiling mad when I look back on it now. I remember drawing maps and reading about grain and hemp (whatever that might be) produced in some strange-sounding places that, supposedly, were part of the same world we lived in. We added and subtracted numbers, diagrammed sentences, saluted the flag endlessly, listened to funny-sounding words from the Bible, lived through various sadistic miseries in gym periods, misspelled words (thereby earning giant red marks), put on plays by mouthing words that we didn't understand, sang songs (I can still remember "Welcome sweet springtime/We greet thee anew . . . "), sounded out words with our mouths while plowing through dull books about happy people who endlessly did happy things, watched the clock until it moved (so slowly) to three o'clock and we were free to leave the school building and brood on our miseries alone, torture one another with mean games, or try to console one another in the treasured moments of friendship.

In the nine years of kindergarten through eighth grade, I learned to read slowly while moving my lips, write almost illegibly (as my Social Security card signed at age fourteen demonstrates), and do arithmetic by counting with my fingers under the table. I also learned to keep my sorrows and my joys secret and I learned patience—if passive waiting is genuine patience. When I think of the real problems of living that my peers and I could have been helped to learn to solve during those years, I am angry about the sad games we played that were called learning. No one is to blame, I suppose. I am sure each of the teachers thought he was doing the best job he could do. But it is so sad to think that all of those human beings were in the same building for all of those years and that that fact was treated as an unpleasant nuisance rather than as the most fertile soil for learning. We could have learned from one another if someone had just started with the assumption that such human learning is possible and respectable!

Growing up in Belmar in those years, it was easy to get a bleak picture of the world and of the people in it. Even when the Depression lifted, it was bad. The winters are bone-chilling in their damp gray cold and the town is filled with people who have nothing to do. They are waiting for summer. The town lives primarily on its one asset, the ocean. In the summer the people from the cities come and bring their money. The summers are spent working long, hard hours doing almost anything that will separate the summer people from their money. The winters are spent in long, dull days dreaming about better ways to separate the summer people from their money. In their winter boredom people deal with one another as if rudely awakened from sleep. They are short-tempered and suspicious. They pick at one another, developing complex rituals of pride that are easily violated, and seem able to cooperate only when they share lustful dreams of the summer to come.

These were the adults who surrounded us as we went through the dull rituals of school learning. When I think about the joyous learning that could have been going on all of those years and the needless agonies that could have been avoided, I would like to bring suit against those people who called themselves my teachers. But what court hears that kind of a case? I know that those teachers, poor creatures, were nothing more and nothing less than the sad products of the same sad "educational" process.

The Japanese bombed Pearl Harbor while I was still in elementary school, and the Second World War entered our small-town American lives. The war continued through most of my high-school years. We were violently patriotic. All of the boys were eagerly waiting to be old enough to join up and there were plenty of stories about how to lie about your age and get in the service early. The war cheered our town a little because it put the enemy clearly "out there" and gave us reason to band together. Living on the coast, we faced the constant danger of being invaded by U-boats, and almost daily someone was fairly sure that he had seen a periscope in the ocean.

One of my brothers went into the Army and found himself in Germany; the other brother was with the Marines in places like Okinawa. My oldest sister even joined the Army and ended up in Fort Sill, Oklahoma. At least she was in uniform! And my other sister went to Washington, D.C., to work as one of the vast corps of anonymous pretty office girls. I was terribly jealous. The glamor of war was everywhere and I was trapped in high school. I worried about my brothers and wrote long cheery V-mail letters that were part of my private war effort to keep up the morale of the troops.

High school was a little more interesting. There were some teachers about whom I was curious. From elementary school I remembered only my kindergarten teacher and my eighth-grade teacher, because I had sensed that both of them liked me (and I had been more than happy to do anything they wanted of me in return for that gift). But in high school there were peculiar teachers who did not fit my preconceived idea of a teacher. There was a freshman

English teacher who was young and cute (!) and yet she really seemed to like books. There was a man who taught Spanish, but who took time out to talk about things like racial prejudice and even mentioned once that his wife was Jewish. There was an English Literature teacher who was divorced and drank too much and could get terrifically carried away while reading *Medea* aloud. She proposed that we each pick some author, any author, and read everything he had written. It is hard to describe how that thought almost blew my mind. I had been going from page to page of required reading for years. I finally picked John Steinbeck because someone said he wrote sexy things; I did actually read all of his books and had perhaps my first educational experience. But high school did not really whet my appetite for learning. It did, however, pique my curiosity enough to start me wondering about college.

I knew that people went to college of their own free will and were not required by law to be there. That, in itself, was interesting. My problem in trying to understand this phenomenon was that I had never met anyone except a teacher who had ever been to college. I certainly could not ask the nitty gritty questions in the back of my mind of some proper teacher, so they went unanswered. I found pictures of a "typical" fraternity house at Yale or Harvard in some magazine like *Esquire*. There were girls and drinking and the whole scene did not look too bad. One of my jobs during high school was working as an usher in a movie theater and I saw Ingrid Bergman and Gregory Peck in the first psychoanalytic movie, *Spellbound*, perhaps twenty or thirty times. It was fascinating that there were such psychological mysteries in people that could be unlocked if you knew how. Obviously this was one of the many mysteries that you could learn in college.

One way or another I had saved enough money to see me through most of one year of college so, with a slightly frightened "what the hell" attitude, I applied to colleges. My grades were good and maybe a few of my teachers had had an eye on me because I was accepted in all but one of the seven colleges to which I applied. I chose Antioch College in Yellow Springs, Ohio, because it had a work-study program; I was not wild about studying, but thought it would be fun to work in various places across the country.

My first few days at Antioch were vivid, eye-opening experiences. First of all, it was not the posh fraternity picture I had seen in *Esquire*, and second, the students were astonishingly friendly. I had grown up in a setting where people would just as soon fight as say "hello," and you lived with your guard up. At Antioch everyone I passed said "hi" and smiled, and it took me a while to relax my paranoid suspicions and realize that these people my own age were genuinely friendly.

The biggest surprise came in a campfire cookout during the Freshman Orientation Week. We sat around singing songs that everyone else seemed to know (I learned later that middle-class youngsters go to camp in the summer). There was a sprinkling of veterans among us, beginning their deferred college years with the G.I. Bill. When it was dark, someone suggested that we break into small groups and talk about what we expected and hoped for in the college years ahead. I found myself in a group of about ten young people who began earnestly to talk about wanting to learn about life and about themselves. They wanted to find books they didn't know about. They wanted to help their fellow man, to stop future wars, to stamp out poverty and disease. They wanted to read and to study! I could not believe my ears. I kept looking around to see if there was a teacher listening. Who were they trying to impress? I don't think I said a word—just sat there and let it sink in that these young people my own age were absolutely serious about wanting to learn. It was a new world that I had stumbled into.

I was a gawky kid with a great shock of unruly hair, plastic-rimmed glasses, and clothes that were too flashy. I ate with the wrong utensils and still said "ain't" sometimes, but I found myself surrounded by friendly people who wanted me as their friend because they could see that they had something to learn from me while I had many things to learn from them. In trying to finance my college education, I was plagued by money problems. I often found myself working at some job when my friends were off playing and I wanted to be with them. But mostly those college years were wonderful stretching and growing years. I was seduced by education. I found there was a marvelous world out there to learn about.

After Antioch there were two dreary years in the Army that I would not want to repeat. These two years did give me unusual opportunities to learn new things about myself and to read books I had not had time for in college (like *War and Peace*). The Army experience helped to convince me of the insanity of war and the near-insanity of the people who staff wars for supposedly good reasons. It helped me to see the wisdom of being a pacifist.

After the Army came graduate school training in clinical psychology. (You see that *Spellbound* had had its effect!) I was still looking for ways to unlock those human secrets. The courses in graduate school were not very rewarding, with a couple of big exceptions. Most of my learning was done on-the-job in the clinical practicum placements, but that may have been my old Antioch work-study orientation showing. I got myself all puffed up with the image of being some professional person known as a "psychologist," and have had to do some heavy relearning in the years since then to shrink myself down to the more satisfying size of a human being.

I had been in psychotherapy myself in the undergraduate years and in group therapy during my graduate school years. I loved learning to be "the doctor" and doing therapy with "my patients." I especially loved learning to do group therapy. But a couple of years after I finished my Ph.D. degree the thrill of being called "doctor" began to diminish. I began to sense that my interests were in the direction of education. I wanted to take something that all of this clinical psychology and psychotherapy had to offer and transfer it into education. I wanted to be with teachers and youngsters. I wanted, of course, a chance to redo my own education vicariously and give the youngsters what I had not had. I wanted young children to see how much fun it can be to learn, and to see that it is fun because, whatever you are apparently learning about or studying, you are always in part learning about yourself and studying your own life.

I took a job as a staff psychologist at the Hunter College Educational Clinic and a few years later moved to the Bronx campus (now Herbert H. Lehman College) as the director of the Educational Clinic there. The clinic had originally been a demonstration child guidance clinic, but we worked in the direction of interesting teachers in understanding what was going on inside of each of them as a human being as a key to understanding how to work with children. We found that watching a youngster undergo psychological testing is an *interesting* experience for a teacher, but grappling with an understanding of how your own emotions interact with the emotions of your students is a *useful* experience for a teacher.

In 1958, I married a girl whom I had met ten years earlier on the train to Antioch. She had gone through the five years there also, and our love had grown out of the closeness of college years. Her name is Barbara and she has beautiful green eyes, a marvelous sense of humor, flair, courage and a great capacity to love. We fight sometimes and say mean things to one another and "have our troubles" but we are very happy to be married and I hope we have a long stretch of years ahead in which we can learn how to love better and how to share more.

We have two children: Vicki, who will be six when this book is published, and Andy, who will be five. I think I have learned more about what it means to love in the few years that they have been with us than I did in all of the preceding years of my life put together. They are now on the threshold of their formal education and that fact both excites and saddens me. The education they will get is still nowhere near the kind I wish I had had myself, yet it is so much closer to that idea than my own early education that it gives me hope for their future.

Asya and I became friends in 1961 when I joined the Educational Clinic staff at Hunter College. Asya had already been there a year as the consultant on groups. You will meet her in her own letter to you, but I want to forewarn you about her ability to cast a spell. I knew within the first few minutes of having met her that we would be friends and that I would grow to love her. She died in 1971 while this book was in the final stages of editing. She had been painfully ill and her death was not truly unexpected but Asya was the kind of person who is so full of life that her death seemed unreal. I miss her cheer and wisdom.

We started on this book about eight years ago. It came about, I suppose, because I noticed that in consulting with teachers in the classroom or talking with them in teacher discussion groups, I found myself saying the same things over and over. I found that I was rarely giving advice that applied to a specific youngster but I was helping the teacher find his or her own perspective and awareness of feelings to use as a key in helping the youngster about whom there was concern. Oh, there were a few words of wisdom about one kind of child or another, but mostly there was this repetition of orientation. In conversations with Asya, I noticed that the same was true for her and we agreed on the content of the repetition. I suppose I was most struck that Asya, with many more years of experience than I, was doing the same kind of repeating. Since I am book-oriented, I thought, "If we are repeating it, we should write it down and let people read it instead of inefficiently using our mouths to say the words over and over." Asya and I had breakfast together once or twice a week for a year with a tape recorder for company. We collected and sorted our thoughts, wrote a first draft of the book (which looked nothing like the present one) and then began the years of rewriting and rethinking. The book was a dream; we did not know if it would ever be published. There have been many pleasant hours together in Asya's sun-filled breakfast room and in my attic study. There have also been hours of grinding work that have not been as much fun. It has been an eight-year pregnancy for this growing book that we conceived and nourished together. We are pleased to present you with our offspring and we hope you like it. We hope it will say to unseen friends who are teachers the same things we have said to our everyday friends who are teachers.

This book is, for me, a living dedication to Asya. It contains so much of her. It seems appropriate that it will be put to use in helping children find richer and more satisfying lives. Asya was not a person whose memory could be captured in a static monument.

Before I close this letter, I ought to describe the *me* of this moment. I am just a shade under six feet tall and I have brown hair that has more than a little grey in it and is cut long. Sometimes I wear body shirts and bells and play hippie but I'm too square to carry it off. There is a noticeable dimple in my chin and my blue eyes turn down a little at the outward corners. There is something about my face that makes people think I'm laughing most of the time, which somehow makes them smile and laugh in response—a nice thing as far as I'm concerned.

I have been having a maddening affair with the typewriter for the past decade. I hate writing, but love it when I have finished writing something. I am pulled between fiction (even published a short story in *McCall's*) and non-fictional educational psychology. I suppose I would like to blend fiction and psychology as Truman Capote (*In Cold Blood*) did with fiction and news reporting.

I still love the ocean. It is the strongest continuing gift from my childhood (unless you can see my need to constantly redo my education as a gift). I go to the beach as often as I can, summer or winter, and spend time walking and looking at the many moods of the ocean. The ocean seems so filled with emotion that changes with little warning, and it is so independent of human joys and troubles and so permanent that it is a marvelous source of perspective and comfort.

My newest professional interest is in the varieties of encounter or sensitivity training, the new movement that is sometimes called the "human potential movement." I have participated in many different kinds of groups and have led encounter groups, and I am terribly excited about the potential they hold for education if we can get the necessary safe bridges built.

Add only that I am in love with young people. The world is changing. Young people are making mistakes but I think they are taking giant steps in claiming the world that can be theirs. They demonstrate an admirable concern for the woes of their fellow humans. It seems to me to be a race between them and the reactionary forces of older generations. But my bet is placed and my fingers crossed. I hope that this book will be of help to the young people who are the teachers of today and tomorrow.

My best wishes,

Don

LETTER FROM ASYA

Dear Reader:

I truly believe as Alfred Adler did, that perceptions of our early childhood determine our goal in life and our basic life-style. I would like to give you a glimpse of my life so that you may better understand my present self.

The fifth child in a family of nine, seven girls and two boys, I was born in Riga of Russian Jewish parents. My earliest recollection is of being in bed in a room full of beds. The one next to mine was empty. It turned out that this was my first experience with death. A younger sister, whom I don't remember at all, had just died of scarlet fever. I wonder whether I am not still reaching out to children in the classroom who seem to be "dead;" they always attract my attention, tugging at my heart.

With my platinum blond hair and fair complexion, I was usually taken for a Christian. The stereotype of a Jewish girl was dark-eyed with black hair. In later years, I let new acquaintances know right away that I was Jewish to avoid hearing anti-Semitic remarks, just as many light-skinned Blacks quickly proclaim their race.

At the age of five, my first day at the government-endowed *gymnasium*, I missed my closest playmate, Ella. I worried all day that she might be sick. I didn't know anyone in the class and was introduced formally only to the teacher. All the girls wore the same brown uniforms with black aprons and we sat on benches facing the teacher's desk.

When our maid called for me after school, my first question was about Ella. She told me that only very smart children were enrolled and only two Jewish children were accepted in each class. I cried all the way home where I announced that I would not go to any school where Ella was not welcome. My mother understood my despair and the next day I was sent to a private *lycée* where Ella was already accepted.

Since my family were of the Russian intelligentsia, their important values were related to how much we children studied, learned and retained. My oldest sister studied medicine; my older brother and next older sister studied engineering. The sister who was four years older than I was a beauty and had no intellectual leanings. She rebelled against the family's values in every possible way, and of course was frequently punished. I furnished alibis for her and actually was her "patsy," for she manipulated me into protecting and shielding her against Papa's harsh treatment. I learned only in my own analysis that my "goodness" was relative to my sister's "badness." I didn't have to rebel in the same way since I could participate vicariously in her thrilling misdeeds without incurring Papa's wrath.

My oldest brother was my ideal. My only academic difficulty was arithmetic. I could call on my brother at any time, and once woke him at 5 a.m. for last-minute help before my third-grade exams. We sat on his bed for an hour or two, going over all the material. He would say, "Asya, pay attention. You're not dumb." Unquestionably I was manipulating him so that I could enjoy his sole company for a couple of hours. I learned through experience that all children probably use "dumbness" to get teachers, parents, and older siblings to give them extra time and attention.

In 1914 when World War I broke out I was a big girl of 12 and usually taken for at least 14. The Jews, as usual, became the scapegoats. Forced out of their homes in Russia, beaten by the Cossacks, they came in droves to Riga, where the local Jews mobilized to provide food and shelter for the dispossessed. About one hundred children and their parents were housed in a big factory outside the city limits. My parents supported my efforts to keep the children reasonably clean, supplying soap, disinfectants and clothing. I had to shave off their hair because of the risk of typhus, and was roundly cursed by their parents who were steeped in superstition and knew little about personal hygiene. Sometimes I felt ten times my age, but my family must have felt that I could "take it" or they would not have approved of the undertaking. I still think there is much to be said for cultures where older children help care for the younger ones. In any event, this was probably the most extraordinary experience of my life and may have determined my choice of profession. My main problem was conveying some notion of hygiene to people who considered the whole idea silly if not dangerous.

I am still interested in working with mothers and fathers in the hope that they can better understand their young ones. During that long summer I learned to take a good deal of strain, some of it due to false accusation and endless hostility, without feeling personally attacked. Little by little, I came to know the pains and pleasures of belonging to a minority group—of being a "good Jew." Like my parents and siblings, I identified partly with the Russian intelligentsia and partly with the world's underdogs: the poor, the oppressed and the persecuted. We all had idealistic goals and were willing to fight for them.

By the fall of 1924, our city was bombarded by the Germans and we moved to Petrograd (later Leningrad) where a new era started for us. I loved Petrograd and, in fact, consider it the most beautiful city in the world. My school was boring, partly because

of my exciting summer "mothering" refugees. I often played
hookey, reading interesting adult books in the parks. And then
came a blow. After doing a lot of research on the subject, I wrote
a paper on the Tartar influence on Russia. When something interested me I went into it wholeheartedly, though I skimmed over less
absorbing subjects. My teacher thought the paper sounded too mature for a school girl and my brother was called in. It was a terrible
shock to have my integrity and honesty questioned, and this is still
true today. Even when my brother made it indisputably clear that
the paper was solely my work, I felt a great sense of personal in-
jury. Even though English was my fifth language, learned when I
was already an adult, I sometimes think my writing block stems
partially from the teacher's false accusation and from my father's
saying that "people should read more and then they would write
less nonsense." It was amazing that my capitalistic parents never ob-
jected to our interest in Marxism, socialism, working in the underground, and belonging to radical groups whose aim was to prepare
for the revolution. They felt that such diversified activities were
part of a total education and helped the growing-up process.

Meanwhile, my sisters returned home. The doctor volunteered
to serve on the Russian-Turkish frontier where epidemics were
rife and medical personnel scarce or non-existent in 1916. While
carrying out her duties on the battlefield and with a high fever due
to malaria, she fell off her horse and died. When my engineer sister
was refused a position in her field because of her sex, she shaved
off her long hair and took a job in a defense plant disguised as a
man—quite a daring maneuver in those long-ago days. Ten months
after my sister's death, my brother was injured while on a government mission and he died following surgery. These were dreadful
blows for all of us.

Next came the Russian Revolution, and fighting was going on
around the corner from our home. It soon became apparent that
our family was in danger and we left for Riga in the middle of the
night with light hand luggage only. No sooner were we back on
the old soil when the Baltic area was invaded by the Germans.
Again we pulled up stakes, this time for Berlin, but none of us
liked Germany.

In 1920 I married the man I loved until death parted us in 1954.
My twin girls were born in 1922. In the following years I attended

universities in Latvia and Vienna part time. Dividing my "spare" time between studying and caring for my husband and children naturally resulted in conflictual feelings, well understood by teachers with families. My father considered psychology too new a science and urged me to go into medicine, but I could not bear the thought of dealing with death, and perhaps meeting it young as my sister had done.

Like many children, I felt that my parents did not understand me, or for that matter, my siblings. True, we were a large, curious-minded brood who would have been a "handful" even for the strongest, best-intentioned, most knowledgable and flexible parents. The fact that they failed to reach us on many levels of our lives enforced my feelings that parents and children *must* come to understand each other more fully. To understand others, I was convinced that I had to know more about myself and the events that had shaped my interests and goals.

When our daughters were three years old, my husband encouraged me to seek more intensive training for my chosen profession. While going through my own psychoanalysis, I took a degree in psychology.

Alfred Adler was probably the most influential person in helping me to crystallize my goals and understand myself and others, providing a real education-in-depth. To my knowledge he was the first psychiatrist with the courage to treat adolescents and their families in the presence of other professionals and students, rather than from behind closed doors, and also the first to shift emphasis from purely verbal communication to nonverbal or "body" language. Although a man of few words, he said things that made everyone listen. The first family I saw him treat consisted of a father, a mother and their young son, Peter, who was about to be jailed for a minor offense. A group of observers, all professionals, were present during the consultation. The parents were very angry with Peter and full of recriminations. He sat hunched over, seemingly oblivious to others. After a while, Adler said, "Peter, what do you plan to do when you get out of jail?" The boy said, "I hadn't thought of it." Adler said quietly, "Well, it's worth thinking about, you won't be there long." The boy straightened up in his chair as if he had gained new courage. (Incidentally, I heard many years later that Peter had become a highly respected physician.) Turning to the audience, Adler then said, "Has anyone here ever been in jail?" Two young men raised their hands, one of whom said, "I learned a lot from the experience, too."

This particular encounter reinforced my desire to work with parents and children. In 1926 I began to lecture and give seminars for parents as well as teachers, traveling throughout the Baltic States, but usually returning home at least every other day. I organized and became director of a large guidance center called "School and Home," similar to the Child Study Association in New York.

A fanatic on the subject of pre-delinquent children from underprivileged families, I converted our home into a haven for them. At one time we had eight youngsters who had been rejected by their various schools for behavior such as stealing, breaking windows, making murderous attacks on classmates or authority figures and committing other serious antisocial acts.

In the early 1930's my husband and I began to consider emigrating to the United States. Death had claimed one of our twins, both of my parents and another brother and sister. Two sisters were already living in New York, where we arrived in May 1940 with our eighteen-year-old daughter. We had high hopes but almost no knowledge of English.

The next few years were difficult in many ways, but rewarding, too. We had to live; we had to learn English; we had to carve a niche for ourselves in a new country. My husband started out wrapping packages in a large bargain store. I seemed to be on a steady lope, working a few hours or days a week in various schools and institutions, trying to learn what made American children tick, and also how to communicate with them in English. I took a job as a housemother in a boys' summer camp and as a consultant in an orphanage, to learn about American child-rearing practices and parent-child relationships. Gradually I became a consultant to numerous schools: Columbia Grammar School, Leonard School for Girls, Dalton Schools, boarding schools such as Cherry Lawn, child guidance clinics, and Kings Country and Bellevue Hospitals where I introduced play therapy and remedial work. I usually served without pay for the first year or so.

We had a tiny two-room apartment on Broadway in the 70's with an extra couch in the kitchen where we often put up European friends who, like ourselves, were trying to learn English, get used to the different customs and establish themselves in their various fields. I turned out to be a poor cook, alas, but anyway had almost no time to think of preparing appetizing meals. We all learned to operate a can opener and were sustained by many excellent canned soups and other foods.

I needed my various jobs to familiarize myself with American educational methods so that I could work in my field of education and psychotherapy. English was quite a stumbling block because I got around to it so late. French, German and Hebrew, in addition to my native Russian, were of little help. Since my various jobs were far-flung, I spent many hours on the subways, where I did my reading, made notes and sometimes had a brief nap.

We were graciously accepted without criticism of our poor language and different European manners. I will always remember an extraordinary experience we had shortly after emigrating. My daughter and I were having ice cream at a drugstore in a small town in upstate New York, chattering away in French. A woman lunching with her daughter at the next table said in correct, American-accented French, "Please forgive me for interrupting you, but I am so glad to hear someone speak the language I love." We talked for a while and when we were about to say goodbye, she invited us and my husband to have dinner with them on the coming Friday, arranging to call for us in her car. Her husband, a well-known psychologist, had taken courses in Paris where she studied music.

We were called for as promised. During dinner I became very anxious. I realized that other guests were invited for the evening and felt sure they were all English-speaking. My vocabulary was very limited, indeed. Soon our hosts and several guests joined in playing beautiful chamber music. A rush of emotion made my eyes fill with tears. It seemed particularly tactful of my hostess to decide that the evening's "communication" would not depend upon our scanty knowledge of English. My own musical family has enjoyed the compositions of Moussorgsky and other Russian favorites, as well as those of French, German and other nationals. If we and our new-found friends shared a love of music, wasn't this a good sign that we would have other mutual interests? I felt fortunate indeed to have met this family who gave me courage and hope.

The next year I was employed on a part-time basis at the Hebrew Orphan Asylum and also at Kings County Hospital, both in

Brooklyn. Our daughter's part-time job waiting on tables was a help to the family budget. We allowed one dollar per day for food at home and about 30¢ each for carfare and lunch. When one of the high school boys at the orphanage saw me eating a sandwich, he said "Why don't you eat with the staff members in the dining room?" No one had mentioned this "fringe benefit" which saved me a few cents a day.

Gradually I started earning a little more in institutional jobs and had a few referrals from colleagues who had known me abroad. Aware of the great lack of understanding between teachers and children, I wondered how the gap could be bridged. I could see that my long-range social goal of fostering adult-child communication, in the home or in the school, had been in process of formulation for a long time.

When I became a consulting psychologist in schools in the New York area, I started working with individual teachers and, when possible, with the parents, trying to inculcate the idea that so-called normal children as well as disturbed ones can be helped only in relation to their environment, which includes parents and teachers or other key figures. I wanted to show that treatment in a vacuum simply does not promote lasting results. I soon started working with teachers in groups in many different schools. In time I became group consultant (with teachers, teachers-in-training, and young children as well as adolescents) at the Hunter College Educational Clinic and later at the new Herbert H. Lehman College in the Bronx. During this period Don Clark and I became friends and collaborators.

My purpose has been to stress the psychological aspects of education and the educational aspects of psychology. At first I concentrated on teacher-child understanding and communication but soon brought in the parents to make their contribution. Teachers had not really made full use of the potential of their ready-made groups, so I emphasized group strength in the classroom. It also enabled me to help teachers understand and cope with their pupils individually and in groups and subgroups in the classroom. Psychologists in education follow different bents, *e.g.*, experimentalists and psychometrics experts. In my case the aim has always been improved understanding between the generations. Since parents and teachers are the adults most closely concerned with the child's growth and development, whatever helps them to do their tasks better seems eminently worthwhile.

For many years now I have developed group therapy and family therapy training and service departments at the Postgraduate Center for Mental Health in New York City and I am very proud that my "baby" can now stand firmly alone. I am equally proud to have provided an Educational Process Workshop for over two decades, a setting in which teachers can freely discuss their classroom problems with others and, in so doing, gain insight into themselves and their own students. I learned and applied principles of group therapy to the field of education.

I hope that some of the concepts in this book will hold meaning for you, the reader.

My best,

Asya

I

School is for People—Big and Small

We hope that this book will be useful to you as a reference book. That is the reason for the detailed table of contents and the reference section at the back. But in order to make best use of any non-fiction book, it is necessary to understand the people who create its recommendations. Our letters in the previous chapter were a start in that direction. This chapter is a second step.

You have some picture of us as individuals and you probably assume that, like all people, we operate on a system of beliefs, prejudices, and assumptions that form our orientation or style. This system could be called a *theory*, but that would be misleading since it does not truly unite related phenomena and offer hypotheses that can be tested.

Our style evolved from our backgrounds, from things that happened to us as children, parents, teachers and, even more, from our training and experience as psychologist-educators. In the latter role, we have been exposed to various psychological theories and research evidence, as well as continued interaction with teachers, parents, and children.

We cannot tell you all of the many influences in our lives (a sad memory from a rainy afternoon in mid-childhood or a moment of colorful decision provoked by a teacher's compliment) and you might not be interested anyway. We *can* try to categorize the detailed factors currently influencing us as practicing psychologist-educators, so that you can better understand why we interact and tackle problems the way we do when we introduce you in the following pages to little children chatting casually about death or older ones hiding secret fears of homosexuality.

We believe that school can be a *people place*, a center where big and small members of the human community learn and live together. The comments that follow say this in detail.

TEACHERS

Teaching is a very human business. In thinking back, we realize that each of our inspiring teachers had some particularly human qualities, not necessarily such assets as warmth and humor, but small indications of human frailty. There was a high-school English Literature teacher who chained-smoked (out of class, of course), wore her hair in disarray, was divorced and drank too much. There was a college history teacher who was overweight, had poor eyesight (with flecks of paint on thick lenses that undoubtedly made his vision even worse); his shirttail was occasionally out or his fly not fully zipped. And there was an eighth-grade teacher whose husband was in a mental hospital and only son was in a reform school—which was enough to make her look unspeakably sad at times. Each of these teachers had a love of learning that they transmitted, yet each was only human: plagued by troubles yet tickled by happenings during the school day, willing and eager to go on with the human experience despite pressing problems.

Each of us has met the "god-teacher" and the "machine-teacher" who never appear reduced to the human condition. They know all the answers and are there to be worshipped or operated with skill. They continue to assume such peculiar roles supposedly because of zeal to inspire learning in the young. But the rewards of human learning are human rewards, and most of us trust those teachers who seem *human* enough to be trusted, emulated or followed.

A common concern of teachers, whether new or experienced, is that some child will ask a question they can't answer. Many of us got the idea in childhood that teachers know all the answers, which is not true by a long shot.

When the red-head with freckles in the third row asks how many miles it is to Mars there is no reason not to tell him if you happen to know. But if you do not know you have your choice of saying, "I don't know but we can look it up together later," or "This is not a good time to ask that because we are talking about another matter. *Let's stick to the theme.*"

Teachers who are unsure of themselves *pretend* to know all the answers, but if a teacher is caught up in the joys of learning and busy formulating new and exciting questions, he is constantly *seeking* answers.

We believe that learning proceeds at a brisk, happy pace when the teacher is aware that he and his students live on a planet in a universe about which very little is known. He does not pretend to be an answer machine, but rather someone whose life work, learning, puts him in a good position to help students learn. He can help them to learn to formulate questions and figure out how to look for the answers. Doing such a job, which only a human can do, gives him the right to the professional title of teacher.

We are not knocking teaching machines or programmed instruction, which are valuable for instruction and practice drill. They can help pupils to build or broaden their vocabularies (*e.g.*, in mathematics and social studies) but not to formulate their own questions or seek the answers. We see programmed instruction not as competition for the teacher but as one of his tools.

Socrates said: "Know thyself," and today's dedicated, young, "groovy" teacher says: "Do your own thing." But you can't do your own thing until you find out what it is, which amounts to finding out a good deal about yourself. Meditative self-exploration is still the basic ingredient, although psychotherapy, sensitivity training, teachers' discussion groups, or a carefully kept diary may prove valuable. All these avenues of exploration can help you observe your feelings and thoughts and resultant behavior more carefully and honestly.

The search is difficult but invariably rewarding. A pretty young teacher who comes to mind had soft soulful eyes and a disarming smile; she thought of herself as loving children and being so understanding that she never became angry. She handed out heavy homework assignments daily "to help her students learn self-discipline." Experience in weekly discussion groups for teachers made her aware that the homework overload was punishment, no more and no less than a swat on the behind of a disobedient child; moreover, it usually followed an incident in which the child's behavior had caused her viscera to churn and her jaw to set firmly. In the long run she realized it was more efficient and honest to let a child know when she was angry, and reserve homework to broaden his learning in some particular area of the curriculum. She found the students were more honest with her the less they had cause to fear her concealed anger and accompanying disguised punishment.

Autocratic methods in the classroom are rarely justified. Since the students are hopefully learning to live in a future democracy, a dictator is the last person in the world to help them gain the know-how. Any parent or teacher at one time or another has had to say: "Please, just do it because I tell you to." If the adult has given ample evidence that he truly has the child's welfare at heart, the child is likely to respond positively, even if reluctantly. But, unless he fears the consequences, why in the world should he trust an adult who habitually says, "Do it because I say so"? How can such an adult help him to grow and understand the complex world in which he lives? We will have more to say about this later since we believe the notion of teaching in a democracy is crucial to the successful teacher-student relationship and to helping teachers cope with the problems encountered in school. Briefly, we are convinced that a person will be a better teacher if he knows himself well and is comfortably at home in a democracy.

It is an unpleasant truth that students in most schools, regardless of chronological age, are second-class citizens. First-class citizenship is available only to administrators, and, in some instances, teachers. A child's regular classroom teacher, of necessity, becomes his unchosen representative in the educational world. Even in a setting where he has other teachers, someone from this small group must represent him.

It is a weighty responsibility to represent someone who did not choose you. Parents have little real opportunity to participate in a youngster's educational experience. During school hours the teacher becomes a parent substitute. A classroom teacher in elementary school or a home-room teacher in high school must represent the youngster's interests in dealing with other teachers, specialists, and administrators, such as the physical education teacher, the remedial reading specialist, and the attendance officer. Small decisions snowball and ultimately steer a child toward a vocational training school or onto a college prep "track."

Blatant slavery has been abolished in our country; perhaps one day students and parents will have more than a token role in educational decisions, but for now the representative teacher must be the educational "master," an unrealistic burden that forces him to walk in the dark and troubled areas. Since he has the best opportunity to know the child as a person, it sometimes means disagreeing with the principal or the objective test results. For example, a quiet scholarly young man whom we know, though in his first teaching year, disagreed with the specialists by insisting that a five-day suspension from school would not help a particular junior-high student learn the value of education or even repent and become more docile, but would merely sentence him to five days on the streets facing survival problems whose solutions are not taught in school. He knew the boy had recently developed a tentative trust in some of his teachers and the "book learning" they offered, and felt that what he most needed at the moment would be five days of more intensive contact with these few teachers. It required a lot of courage for this teacher to demand a "hearing," but he considered it his responsibility as the boy's teacher-spokesman; to duck it would mean selling out the boy's trust or compromising his own professional self-respect.

We are not kidding ourselves and do not mean to kid you. Plenty of people in the profession are in no way worthy of the title of teacher. Historically in our culture, teaching has more often been a job than a profession, but we feel hopeful that the serious attempts now being made to turn it into a first-rate calling can be successful, though it will take a lot of pooled efforts. Lack of professionalism is easy to spot in almost any school. A mild form is the two teachers in the classroom doorway gossiping about the children imprisoned within the room. We do not refer to a serious exchange of information that could benefit the child, but rather to such tidbits as: "I heard his mother is living with another man, but what can you expect?" or "Her father is one of those agitators, always picketing for something." The very same gossipy teacher may wonder why the parents have not trusted him sufficiently to confide that the child shows some evidence of brain damage, or that an impending divorce may cause some emotional reaction in the child which will be noted in school. Even genuinely professional teachers will be treated warily until they have proved themselves or until many of the babysitting wage earners have been weeded out of the school systems. The sad fact is that teachers must expect, for the time being, to meet with a lack of trust from parents and professionals such as the family doctor and school psychologist.

The better you are in touch with your own feelings and fantasies, the more often you bump into a curious phenomenon among your co-workers. The staff of a school resembles a family, though more often a camp version of a Victorian family than a swinging twentieth-century one. It's strange how easily you can be caught up in small struggles, cross-currents or infatuations with colleagues because someone insists on being your stern daddy, kindly aunt, or sister-rival, and because of your own early family relationships you get sucked right into his game. That would be interesting and perhaps amusing except that it can influence your peace of mind and your students' well-being. A student may say: "You told me it's better to study a little bit every day, but Mr. Whatchamacallim says to study hard just before exams so you'll remember more." It is hard to realize that your sibling competition with Mr. Whatchamacallim is involved, that the student realized it before you did, and that the student should not be caught in the middle. If you can make the association promptly, of course, you can explain why you prefer the day-to-day study method, then advise him to listen to all sides of an issue before making his decision. The ghosts of teachers' and administrators' early familial relationships create too many rivalries and other games hurtful to the students.

Survival tools can help a teacher. We believe that *humor, excitement,* and *perspective* are all-important to the teacher's optimal daily functioning and represent his "survival tools." Humor and excitement of the more profound variety (as opposed to the pale substitutes in TV situation comedies) tend to lead logically to perspective which in turn may foster learning. A class without these ingredients is frighteningly unreal. Students must simply survive it until they can return to the real world which is rich in both. Because many of them have been led to believe that school is a dull place where dull teachers supervise dull hard work, the excitement level sometimes drops dangerously low and a teacher has to administer a shot: "If you could learn only one more thing in your whole life, what would it be?"

The kind of humor that can broaden the perspective may arise in the most unlikely happenings. For example, when a third-grade boy yelled out: "I don't want to sit next to Fernando; he got born without no hand and he's a freak," the situation was not really funny but had its elements of humor. What if the teacher had the perspective of a being from another planet observing the scene from beyond the clouds. Imagine! With all the real battles for survival this species might be fighting or training their young to fight, one small animal does not wish to sit next to another one with a missing hand. It is an important event, of course, like all other things that happen between two classmates, especially if one of them may suffer damage to his self-image as a result. Such a small thing, or even reference to it, can cause a deep hurt. We know a teacher who threw in a distraction by saying: "What kind of nonsense it this? I hope we have better ways of deciding whether we like each other than how our bodies are put together. My ears happen to stick out and I wear glasses, but shouldn't you have better reasons for turning me in for another teacher?" In his own natural way, this teacher was trying to get the pupils to see the humor in this tragic incident, thereby increasing their perspective and potential for learning.

It is admittedly difficult to master individual and group problems in the classroom, so it's well to remember that you can request help. There is, of course, no substitute for first-hand detective work in your own classroom and you may feel, perhaps rightfully, that you know the children better than an "outside" specialist, but just the same, call for help when you need it. In most contemporary school systems various specialists are at hand or on call. Some are incompetent but you can soon spot which ones are useful. They may include the guidance counselor, the school nurse, the school psychologist, the curriculum coordinator, the attendance officer, the dean of discipline, the principal, the assistant principals, the remedial reading teacher, the speech teacher, the music teacher, the art teacher, the physical education teacher, the science teacher, and perhaps even the school physician or nurse, a social worker, or a psychiatrist.

It is easy to lose sight of the expert status of the classroom teacher, who must understand each pupil well enough to know when to call on specialists and to evaluate and coordinate their efforts in his behalf. A complicated kind of expertise is required of the classroom teacher; no book can help you find your way around among the particular experts available in your school. The labels do not always mean the same thing. A school psychologist in one place

may spend most of his time administering and interpreting personality tests, achievement tests, vocational interest tests and academic
achievement tests while, in another place, he may spend most of
his time giving clinical assistance to emotionally disturbed youngsters and vexed teachers. You'll have to keep an ear to the ground
to find out how each of the associated specialists defines his professional responsibility.

The following is a case in point: Joan's parents were asked by
the principal and classroom teacher to see the school's consultant
psychologist. Both parents and teacher thought he would be testing
Joan and would need factual information including such details as
her adoption. When he told them he already knew a great deal
about the child, including the fact that she was adopted, had observed her in the classroom, and discussed her problems with the
principal and her teachers, the parents were more than surprised.
When the consultant wanted to explore the parents' feelings and
the home climate, they were reluctant to "give," indicating that the
child's problems at home were not related to school and each should
be handled separately. Had the teacher been more aware of how
this specialist operated, the parents could have been better prepared
and the specialist better used.

Some specialists are not much help to a teacher. They view their
roles and functions in the school system differently. One teacher
said: "Those 'experts' think they know more about the child in one
hour than I do after having him in my classroom for three months.
Besides they give me a run-around. The guidance counselor sends
me to the psychologist and he sends me right back. I don't have time
to gallivant around all day and in the long run they are of no help
anyway."

In this book we try to approach a youngster's problems largely
from the teacher's point of view. With some variation, however,
parents as well as the guidance counselor, principal, physical education teacher, and other specialists may find the same suggested
framework useful for understanding the problems and working
toward a constructive resolution.

If taken seriously and viewed professionally, no job is as appall-
ingly demanding or as fully rewarding as that of a committed
teacher. Teachers, who can save future generations from annihila-
tion or dumb animal existence are paid much less than physicians

who save lives from time to time. It would be funny if it were not so sad.

STUDENTS

Being sufficiently receptive to another person to experience and appreciate him fully is just as hard as, or even harder than, understanding oneself fully. We have pointed out that teaching demands a complex interaction between one human being (yourself) and many others (your students). Every teacher has attended psychology lectures on individual differences but they seldom had much meaning since they stressed the person as an object and left the interacting observer (yourself) out of the picture entirely.

We often make the mistake of assessing a student by his progress toward the goal we think he ought to have, or in relation to standards and values we have overtly or covertly set for him. We fail to understand him in terms of the direction toward which his own unique needs, goals, and values are steering him. Young people, while impressively individual, are more alike than different. Unless seriously damaged, each is trying to find his place in the sun. He may not be well-motivated for school work, as we define it. He may not aspire to a college education. But he does seek a "better" life. He is often unsure of just how he would like to improve his life because he lacks sophistication, but a teacher open to him and his needs can help him clarify his goals. He is apt to play dumb with a teacher trying to sell him goals that don't feel right because they don't fit his life-style. He will nod agreement and pretend to go along, but since his only investment in the project is to keep the salesman-teacher off his back, he continually "fails."

Each of us has enough perception to understand another person to some degree, or to try to slip into his shoes. We fall short of open participatory interaction because we are too quick to resort to shallow but handy answers to the questions that nag us about another person. A good test of how well you understand someone is your reaction to his behavior when it puzzles you in some way. As you try to understand his reasons you are tempted to say: "His actions must mean that he feels such and such a way." No matter how logically correct and sound, your theory represents incomplete understanding unless you can *feel* and identify with the other person. We are not talking about understanding with your head, but feeling the rightness of his behavior in your guts. When you think that in his shoes you would do the same thing because there seems to be no choice, you have tuned in on his wavelength and can identify with him. But you still need to check and recheck to find out his own true feelings and meanings. Most of us at that point say to ourselves: "But maybe what he's doing isn't right. What if he gets into trouble or hurts others?" These are moral questions to be considered *after* you have gained understanding of the person. They are reasonable questions and must be answered, but we tend to let them intrude *before* we understand him. Too often they frighten us away from trying to get inside his thoughts and feelings, in which case we may offer advice on matters of grave importance to someone we do not know nearly well enough.

TAKE THEM AS THEY COME

Despite knowing better, we may jump all over a high school or college student who begins to relate experiences with drugs such as acid or speed. Too often, instead of keeping our mouths shut and ears open as he tries to reveal himself, we hear ourselves spouting about drugs being dangerous to play around with because of the chance they'll mess up his body and mind, in addition to being against the law. When we check this impulse, however, we can go along with the student, appreciate him as a person and understand, among other things, the meaning of the drug experience in his life. If he asks for advice, we give it; he may even listen with interest if he senses that we appreciate and understand him. Gratuitous advice merely conveys the idea that we want him to be different and can't appreciate him as he is.

This process of opening up to another person is related to what psychologists call "acceptance," which somehow sounds unfortunately condescending. It is not a matter of grandly tolerating someone, but of trying to overcome a tendency to consider things that do not fit your own value system or life style as dirty or wrong. In today's language you must be able to "dig" the other person's "thing" or you are not "grooving" or even genuinely "rapping" with him. The current teenage vocabulary is lingering a long time, probably because our "proper" language does not easily express this kind of profound acceptance and understanding which is better understood by under-thirty than over-thirty citizens.

Anna, in the musical *The King and I,* had a clue to all of this when she sang "Getting to Know You." A teacher who found herself with children in a foreign culture, she knew that understanding of each other would have to come before school learning. The song explains that to get to know others, you begin by being honest about your own thoughts and feelings; also that your "right," "wrong," "good" or "bad" reactions to their revelations will inhibit their ability to show themselves fully to you.

LIFE STYLE

Each youngster has a life style of his own, a pattern that fits him. One may reach out to touch everything in the world around him, or run eagerly toward any new experience. Another may hide, keeping his body out of touch with anything new. Still another seems to go around in circles, never moving out to meet the world, never hiding from it, but not being touched by it either. It is difficult for a teacher to achieve genuine respect for each child. We all have our sore spots or blind spots (such as a too-quick reaction to the mention of drugs). And our culture has its blind spots, too. We have learned not to try to make left-handed children right-handed, but we still find it hard to respect a relatively introverted child in our outgoing twentieth-century American culture. In a learning atmosphere someone may change without feeling any demand on him to do so.

DEVELOPMENT OF TRUST

Rapport is based on a delicate and intricate framework of trust that develops slowly. In some school settings the courtship that leads to open understanding is especially delicate. Black ghetto children, for good and sufficient reasons, seldom open their hearts to, and share their thoughts and experiences with, a white teacher associated with other white authorities and thus viewed as a potential threat. A black teacher in a white class would face the same kind of problems, for different reasons. In these courtships, the teacher is asked to pass so many extremely grueling tests of loyalty and friendship that he may fail, and the students thus cannot open up and begin to trust him.

Unfounded assumptions about a youngster are certain to slow down or block the development of his trust. Assuming that every child in your class has a mother, a father and a happy, well-ordered home can convince a child living in a foster home or a fatherless home that you can't see the real him. A pleasant first-grade teacher goofed badly in an attempt to reach out to a pupil who had often been late for school because his older brother and sister didn't start from home on time. After a massive effort that included childish bribes and threats, the first-grader managed to get them up earlier and to school on time one morning. The teacher, thinking he deserved some recognition, wrote across the entire front blackboard, "JIMMY NEWTON IS HERE ON TIME THIS MORNING—CONGRATULATIONS." She undoubtedly thought the public recognition would please him, but might have realized that he merely wanted to blend in with his peers instead of sticking out like a sore thumb each morning. He looked on her "reward" as a cruel humiliation, an attempt to make fun of him, and never trusted her after that. She had made an unwarranted assumption about him before she had begun to know him and his environment.

The building of trust is terribly important; it not only lets two people open up to each other, leading to genuine mutual understanding and appreciation, but also is an essential ingredient in the growing-up process. A reservoir of trust permits bursts of initiative leading toward autonomy. A healthy human being usually develops a respectable-sized reservoir of trust in the world around him while still in infancy. Sensible parental protection has made him believe that the world is not a particularly harmful place. Many people do not store up much trust during infancy, and later experiences sometimes deplete their slight reservoir. A growing child needs a lot of reassuring relationships to keep the reservoir full so that he is able to reach out into the world and to develop his initiative. Continued use of initiative brings him closer and closer to autonomy as he grows up.

The autonomy he seeks is not *independence*, since in our social civilization no one is truly independent of others. He bungles and fails in attempting to stand on his own feet, but usually learns from his failures. He loses his way at times, and when the trust reservoir is dangerously low his growth may be arrested temporarily or, if the level remains low too long, become twisted and take unfortunate forms that will adversely affect his adult life. But through it all, like some magnificent character in a comic strip, our hero continues to grow and move closer to autonomy. Any parent, teacher, or friend who can understand and appreciate him as an individual will be called on to help him along the way.

Attempts of teachers and parents often fail because it is hard to meet someone's dependency needs (*e.g.*, restocking of the trust reservoir) while at the same time fostering his need for autonomy. Ideally the adults should be naturally intuitive or psychologically sophisticated or both; unfortunately, many are neither. The youngster is saying: "I need you to lean on now but don't try to hold me back." That is quite a challenge whether the youngster is two or twenty. The two-year-old may sit happily in your lap one minute and yowl the next minute because you won't let him grab his playmate's toy truck. The twenty-year-old may complain one day that you're too busy to spend time rapping with him and getting to know him better, and complain the next day that a school project (if you are his teacher) or a family outing (if you are his parent) will keep him from a date or a night out with the boys. His complaints and requests make good sense if you understand what he is trying to accomplish.

When something goes awry in the growth process of a particular student, a teacher will want to take an especially careful look at him. This involves more than full appreciation and understanding. If things are going well in your teaching experience but your repeated attempts to slip into the youngster's shoes have somehow failed, it may be *your* hangup. If it is his, he may need some special help. Careful observation requires skill as well as kindness and understanding. Unsuccessful attempts at a genuine relationship may result in bruised feelings on both sides that are all too likely to cause one to misread the evidence.

SIMILARITIES AND DIFFERENCES

The question to keep in mind when making official observations is: "How is this youngster different and how is he like other youngsters of approximately the same age, development level and subculture?" The published psychological and physiological norms are of little use to a teacher because the young people in each class set their own norms. You will want to compare this particular young-

ster with others growing up in the same neighborhood and part of
the country, and it may be useful to guess about the quality and
quantity of trust in his reservoir and about how far along the road
to autonomy his thrusts of initiative have carried him.

We usually start by taking a careful look at the youngster's
body, basic equipment for interacting with his world, which has
much to do with the kind of information he can gather. We try to
assess his vision, hearing, and sense of touch, all of which are crucial in his school activities. His senses shape his understanding of the
world. If he is acutely sensitive in a certain area the world may rush
in on him faster than he is able to assimilate it. A dulled sense, on the
other hand, may make it hard for him to establish firm contact with
the world around him.

BODY LANGUAGE AND NONVERBAL COMMUNICATION

Because of our own experience in human relations, another person's body speaks to us almost like abstract poetry if we are open to
messages. We know that the world responds differently to the fat
and the thin, and we even know some of the reasons why people eat
too much. We get similar messages by noticing whether the person
is relatively tall or short, heavily muscled or flabby, has oily skin or
dry, has much or little body hair, has fine or coarse, curly or straight
head hair. We get messages from eyes which may be alive and danc-
ing or dull and hooded. Large or small ears, flanged or set close to the
head, may be clean or dirty. We observe whether the face is animated
or mask-like, the hands strong or delicate, the stance assured or tentative. We note any deformity or irregularity such as a cleft lip or
palate or a very large nose; a forward posture that would seem to
propel the person to his next encounter, or a leaning back as if he
were afraid; a fast determined walk or a lethargic dispirited movement toward or away from others, or lack of awareness of them.
We especially notice how he habitually establishes contact with
aspects of his world—with his eyes, hands, feet, or ears. Prejudice
often centers around physical characteristics such as a long nose or
tightly curled hair. The film *The Two of Us* brought out compel-
lingly the French peasant's anti-semitism, and his dismay when the
little Jewish boy linked the old man's facial characteristics to the
group he held in contempt.

Notice the clothing next. It may be attractive or unattractive,
apparently chosen with care or thrown together, expensive or inex-

pensive, threadbare or serviceable; in any event, it sends its own messages about the wearer's world. We also like to see the person move among a group and among physical objects both indoors and outdoors, playing, walking, and working. We listen to his voice: high pitched or low, pleasant or harsh, sounding angry or docile. We notice his choice of words: vague or precise, poetic or impoverished expressions, the presence of a dialect or typical inflection, or foreign accent, and particularly his gestures and inner responses which are learned and introjected from infancy.

We like to see how he gets along with his peers, and to spot his usual role—buffoon, oracle, radical, errand boy—noting whether he carries it with ease. We look for his close friends and try to see if he feels more comfortable in a small or large group. We are interested in whether he likes a small or large group. We are interested in whether he likes being a boy (or she likes being a girl). Does he do better with or without supervision? We hope clues picked up from observing him with peers will reveal how he gets along with siblings and parents, though we can probably obtain more direct information about that.

It is impossible to list all of the clues we hunt for, but like the novelist, we must take care not to overlook significant details lest we miss the essence and end up with a two-dimensional character. The overall question is: "What kind of a person is this youngster becoming?" When you have begun to answer it you may find out why your attempts to form a satisfying relationship with him have failed. You may have some quirk that makes you shy away from a person of his kind, or his development (physical or psychological) may have taken a peculiar twist that makes him unhappy. If that is the case, you may be able to suggest help from some source (including parents, other grown-ups in his orbit, and older siblings) and/or do something yourself to set his feet on his chosen path. The teacher and student need each other's help for this task.

SCHOOL

Change is in the air, as always, but the wind is blowing faster these days because of the groundswell for action *now*. Even that sluggish animal we call the American educational system is probably going to shake a leg during the remaining decades of the twentieth century. It has always been adept at changing styles with the times but the public is now demanding that it trim off the fat, question its fondest self-concepts, and find out the sort of work for which it is best suited. We will very likely have to relinquish the idea of a system that dishes out identical educational meals for all students. Viewing one school at a time, we may have to keep track of which students need a hot and spicy curriculum, which ones need to remain on a bland diet for the moment, and which ones are capable of doing their own educational "cooking" with some guidance. Not every child in the nation will learn to spell the word *together* during the third grade, but then they never did. Most of the third-grade teachers have made an effort to teach this spelling but the children, always individualists, had to learn things important to *them* at the moment, such as rocket launchings from Cape Kennedy or the secret sexual practices of adults.

INNOVATIONS IN SCHOOLS

Long overdue changes in the nineteenth-century concept of a school have already been made. Some classrooms now have movable furniture because children need to move. Schooling may take place in the park, the parking lot, or the playground. Some schools are in storefronts or basements rather than awesome old stone castles or modern complexes of brick boxes, glass cages and interconnecting mazes. School buildings may even have movable partitions instead of walls; in some schools, sound-absorbing ceilings, walls and carpeting designed to keep the noise level bearable for adults and working children have replaced thick stone walls, closed doors and detention halls.

But too often architectural innovations precede innovations affecting the teacher and principal. In a flashy, flexible new building, children still may be grouped by chronological age into homogenous classes under the supervision of one teacher for a year or a daily period, as they were fifty years ago. The new architecture simply imposes an additional strain on teachers and students since they have to build invisible walls and doors for their classes and restrain their own voices to shut out interesting diversions in nearby areas. The building is meant to encourage flexibility but in practice it may succeed only in making old rigid ways doubly difficult to pursue.

Then there are schools, unfortunately few and far between, where a child can move from teacher to teacher and group to group as his educational needs change. And there are schools, also rare, where one teacher specialist handles all of the programmed instruction, books, films and other media for a particular area of the curriculum, while other teacher-specialists fill the role of stimulant, comforter, perspective-builder, mother-substitute or general educational guide to small groups of children. Certain schools boast of ungraded classes, flexible programming and interest in development of the total child, but closer examination reveals that they have added window dressing and new words to describe the same old product.

SYSTEMS THRIVE ON CONFORMITY

We believe it is too difficult for a large school system to meet the needs of individuals. That goes for teachers and administrators as well as students. Youngsters and adults are taught their roles and discouraged from side-stepping the rules of the various games played because such nonconformity or deviance, though a valuable aid to individual learning, fouls up the system. If people begin to do the unexpected, what will happen tomorrow? A young man in your class may be turned on to the idea of discovering what kind of education was available in Africa before the slave trade started. It would be an interesting research project clearly related to his present needs, but he would have to do it in his spare time as a special project, if at all, because if he doesn't learn more about the history of his own state with the rest of the class he never will pass the yearly statewide exams. That is, in a nutshell, the story of the conflict between meeting individual educational needs and serving the needs of the system.

A young teacher felt that having her tenth graders use her first name might narrow the communication gap between them. Then she learned that it would be considered "poor educational practice" by the Board of Education. Besides, that young man with a beard tried it two years ago and *he* left school under something of a cloud. She wanted to try something possibly offering her and the students a chance to break an old psychological set and to *learn*, but the system's answer was: "Don't rock the boat. We have enough troubles now; something new might add more woes and make it even harder to maintain our system." You can see why we do not believe that the two words *educational* and *system* live comfortably together.

We are painfully aware of the fact, however, that almost all teachers today are part of an educational system and must find ways within it to work with youngsters' problems and facilitate learning. The system makes the job harder or, to use that educational euphemism, more *challenging*, but it still can be done. We hope today's teachers will demand action leading to abolition of educational systems, but meanwhile, back in the schoolhouse, our approach to problems has been developed, for better or worse, within these confines.

Some changes are being made in the time-honored (but untested) context of the school system's rules, regulations and customs. The time of a school-castle separated from the rest of the community is long past, and a good thing, too. The school is there to provide an education that will fit a youngster to take part in the real world when he grows up. It's foolish to think that a make-believe world with paper pumpkins on the window, where controversial topics are avoided, can possibly prepare anyone for creative participation in the red-hot world. Voices from the children's own neighborhood must be heard in the school. They may demand a change in the status quo or that things be kept as they are. The subjects may include politics, prejudice, anger, and concern for a better world; students, regardless of age, must begin to weigh the arguments advanced and be helped to draw their own conclusions.

PARENTS

In our zeal as parent-surrogates with responsibility for our students' welfare, we sometimes get carried away to the point of protecting them from the real parents. Wrought-iron fences, locked doors and school visitation rules intimidate many parents into feeling that they must hand over their children *in toto* from Monday through Friday, and that it would be impertinent to seek a voice in school matters. On the other hand, many parents in public as well as private schools are demanding and receiving a big voice in matters both curricular and extra-curricular.

How often have teachers said and heard colleagues say: "Parents are a nuisance. They barge into the classroom, interrupt and disturb the teaching process. The children try to 'show off' and besides, it makes me uncomfortable. They watch me like a hawk and I wonder if they're planning to complain to the principal or PTA about me."

We were chatting with a fifty-two year old teacher recently just before her scheduled conference with a twenty-nine-year-old mother. "I know why she wants to see me," the teacher said. "Jerry's probably told her all the kids tease him and that I've been assigning too much homework. I try my best to keep him out of trouble but he has a real talent for getting everyone's goat." As her monologue continued, it became clear that she was preparing herself, in fantasy, for mama's criticism by finding excuses that might lessen the mother's anger.

It is ironic but understandable that teachers and parents so often seem at odds when both apparently have the youngster's welfare at heart. All parents have had some teachers who acted with unreasonable authority and all teachers have some unresolved differences with their own parents. Since parent and teacher usually wear invisible signs (I AM A PARENT; I AM A TEACHER) and approach the meeting with some trepidation, each expecting to defend his authority, genuine rapport may be hard to achieve. The teacher reacts partly as he did to his own parents while the parent reacts partly as he did to his own early teachers. It is as tempting for teachers to blame parents as for parents to blame teachers, since both are reacting to fear of accusation, but the youngster is inevitably caught in the crossfire between these two powerful forces in his life.

MUTUAL RECRIMINATIONS

When parents and teachers list their dissatisfactions with each other, we are often struck by the childish tone of the complaints. An irate mother says, "Marianne's teacher used a lot of fancy words to say she wasn't doing too good because she must be having some trouble at home. So I said it seemed fishy that the trouble at home started just when *she* replaced the teacher who left in the middle of the year. She said she wasn't having any trouble with the other kids, and I said maybe she wasn't watching them so closely." The equally irate teacher tells a co-worker, "I wouldn't give her the satisfaction of saying I don't know what's the matter with Marianne when she wasn't even courteous enough to thank me for calling the problem to her attention."

Not a day goes by in the school without a hassle developing because a teacher or a parent feels he has been misunderstood or treated unjustly. In our experiences, all teachers feel burdened—whether with blame, guilt, personality differences, their own conflicts and ambivalent feelings, or struggles with the hierarchical system. We believe they can be greatly benefited by workshops conducted perhaps once a week by a perceptive and well-trained leader from the outside. Such workshops enable the teacher to ventilate his own feelings and, with the help of his peers, sort out his "beefs" and realize what is being projected onto the parent or the child, what is personal and what is objective. He also obtains valuable suggestions from colleagues and workshop leaders on means of tackling specific situations. Don't miss the opportunity to have such a workshop in your school; you have a right to demand it. We have conducted successful workshops at lunchtime between bites. The set-up can be strictly informal; all that is needed is a place and time for the teachers to meet with a leader to air problems, preferably at least once or twice a week.

Parents seem to be the teacher's most frequently forgotten educational resource. Almost all parents are interested in their child's welfare but may express their interest in ways that do not fit your own educational values or actual experience with the child. It is worth remembering that of the two, you are supposedly the trained professional and must assume the professional responsibility for converting common interest in the child into team work. You cannot indulge in controversy and still meet your responsibility. You must take the parent as is and use him to the best possible advantage in the task of educating his child. Your primary concern is not whether he appreciates how hard you work and how talented you are, or even whether he is a "fit" or "nice" or even "moral" parent, but how he can help the team effort.

There is no denying that it's gratifying to have a college student or a kindergartner look you square in the eye and say, "I wish you were my father," or "Why can't my mother be like you?" but we have to remind ourselves that we are only substitute parents for part of the day. The youngster returns to his real parents day after day, year after year, and we must be careful to strengthen what is potentially helpful in his relationship with them instead of weakening the bond to fulfill our ego needs of the moment.

When a parent reads a report card he usually feels that the parents and the home, as well as the child, are being evaluated. It is a hard job to be a full-time parent and most of us have had little educational preparation for it, as we both know very well. Says Don: "When my oldest child started nursery school at the age of three, I could hardly wait to sneak in gracefully as an observer. I really wanted to see how she was holding her own in this new world, compared to other three-year-olds, raised by perhaps more competent, patient, understanding or inspired parents. I saw and heard all that went on (and reminded myself that I am a teacher of teachers) but still was terribly relieved to hear the teacher say, 'Vicki really seems to be enjoying school lately.' Later the anxiety set in as I carefully examined each treasured word. What had she meant by 'lately?' Was there some trouble before? I noticed that Vicki spent a lot of time on the climbing apparatus and wasn't much interested in the dress-up corner of the kitchen. Was she finding it difficult to relate to other children and the teacher had not wanted to mention it? Fortunately, it was a cooperative nursery school and my wife spent the whole morning there every few weeks. She reassured me there had been nothing wrong earlier; 'lately' is one of those words people add to sentences to make you feel they are communicating about the here and now."

Says Asya: "I also recall my anxiety every time I was called for a report card conference at my daughter's progressive school. The report card was never sent home; I was given it to read during the first five minutes of the conference. Of course, I got hung up on some sentence such as 'Sary is too playful' and became anxious about whether the teacher loved and appreciated my little girl. I constantly looked for a glowing appraisal and feared criticism of her and of my way of raising her. Once a teacher's remark, 'You're a psychologist; you ought to know better!' demolished my ego completely."

Our experience reveals that the more important the parent's position, the more likely he will show anxiety by strongly criticizing or attacking the teacher. Interestingly enough, neither the teacher's age nor experience makes much difference in the parent's approach. You hear a black parent complain, "Miss B. is white and she is prejudiced against my Jimmie because he is black." Down the hall a white parent says, "Miss J. (a black teacher) doesn't like Mary;

she's envious because Mary is so fair, blonde and blue-eyed. She wishes she could have looked like her." If only Miss J. could tell the parents that she had struggled for days over the report card. The chairman of her department went over it with a fine-toothed comb; then the principal commented on it. But the parents may say that she wasn't fair because they had a lingering suspicion that Miss J. didn't really know the child and was prejudiced against her. It is well for the teacher to keep in mind that parents may have the same paranoid feelings about teachers of the *same* race, color, religion, and social status.

A parent who is overly concerned about everything is likely to take all of a teacher's comments too seriously. You get the feeling that their entire home life would be re-arranged if you were merely to give an overt or covert signal. Words that pass from teacher to parent must be carefully weighed since they may be misinterpreted. You may have the best intentions in the world when you say, "I'm surprised to hear that you're having trouble with Felix at home because I haven't noticed anything out of the way at school." The parent's interpretation may be that you are competent and he is not, since you can handle problems that floor him. If you help to make a parent feel incompetent he cannot be very helpful to his child. It's far better to bolster whatever strengths you find in him and request his help in the educational team effort.

FATHERS TO THE FORE

This may be a good place to recommend that you do what you can to break the vicious circle that excludes fathers from active interest and participation in their children's educational experiences. The subtle rejection is everywhere, starting with the mimeographed notes that read, "Mothers are invited to make appointments for conferences with the teachers . . . "or "Mothers' study group will meet . . . " The poor father is paid lip service only; he is assumed to be too busy earning the family living to participate in school affairs. The message is perfectly clear to any neglected father, and the child is bound to share our attitude toward him. If everyone in the educational establishment really believed fathers should be involved, parent-teacher conferences could be arranged in the evening for fathers who are not free during the day. That once-a-year "Fathers' Night" show doesn't convince anyone that educators really want to hear from this group. We may deplore Momism in our society, but we encourage it by preventing fathers from taking an active interest in the school community. "Mother knows best" is such a common phrase; do we truly believe that women are more important than men as parents—or teachers?

DISCIPLINE

Any large institution must cope with the problem of control. In schools the word *control* seems distasteful and has yielded to misleading labels such as "civic responsibility," "learning," and "discipline." We will have more to say on this subject but want to point out early that we see the institution's problem of control as legitimate but quite different from the individual's problem of discipline.

In most dictionary definitions, *discipline* has a connotation of punishment for purposes of correction and training, yet the word comes from *discipulus* (a disciple) and *discere* (to learn). Any school worth its salt is interested in the transformation or development of character. We are convinced that a school should aim for development of the self-discipline that facilitates a youngster's ability to think, to plan, and to use freedom with an increasingly discriminating sense of responsibility. Self-discipline can become the means of feeding a healthy intellectual curiosity.

We believe teachers should be as conscious of goals for character development as of academic goals. Childish patriotic frills such as pledging allegiance to the flag in a morning chorus of misunderstood words or singing about bombs bursting in air have nothing to do with character development. Self-discipline as a means toward this goal implies understanding and accepting the fact that one cannot escape the consequences of his actions. It is a good idea for any growing person to ask himself from time to time what he wants to become and whether his behavior is helpful toward this goal. Also, does his behavior please himself and others or is a change of attitude indicated? As he grows older he may ask, "What kind of a world do I want to live in? Can I help shape it?" And "Why do I behave this way?" Obviously he gets some primary or secondary rewards, either positive or negative. For example, the class clown is sometimes a trial to the teacher but his peers are usually enchanted; and the boy who throws spitballs, "sasses" the teacher, and makes annoying remarks to the girls, would stop if he weren't getting some attention he craves. At the end of the school year, the student may ask, "In what way am I more grown up than I was last fall?" The only yardstick worth much is his past performance—a comparison of "me with me," not "me with others." All of this is intimately related to *discere* (to learn). If we teachers would apply the same kind of soul searching and growth evaluation to ourselves, we would undoubtedly see more of the *discipulus* (disciple) part of the root of *discipline*.

SETTING LIMITS

It seems necessary for a school as an institution to try to establish appropriate limits, rules and regulations. A teacher or administrator should have no more guilt about establishing ground rules early in the year than a youngster should have about rebelling against them or over-stepping them now and then.

When rules are based on sound reason and students have actually helped to formulate them, overstepping or rebelling is usually confined to individual students trying to learn on their own about self-control versus outside control. There are real reasons why teachers and administrators must insist on some rules, even though someone will always rail against them. They are needed, for example, to protect individual citizens from bodily harm. Even very young pupils usually see the need for rules as clearly as any administrator, if given the chance to hash them out thoroughly beforehand.

Asya says: "When I was consulting psychologist for a junior high school, one classroom was plagued by a series of small thefts, especially money or objects taken from the teacher's pocketbook on her desk. She finally said, 'I'm not at all happy about living in a community, like our classroom, where I can't even leave my pocketbook unguarded for a moment. What kind of citizens are we, anyway? I look on you as my friends and hate to think at least one of you doesn't consider me his friend.' A pupil waved his hand for attention. 'I get it,' he said, 'if you're going to steal, don't steal from someone you live with. Go someplace else.' There was much more learning to be done here but the petty thievery stopped permanently."

We cannot expect bigger miracles for the young than for adults. A student runs afoul of the rules now and then, but if he and his peers have helped to make them it is easier to turn transgression into a learning experience reinforced by his peers. Learning to regulate our own behavior and control our own impulses is a hard job; most of us are still trying to achieve self-discipline. Any student who has developed better self-discipline within the past few months, even if he's no paragon, is probably doing better than most of us are.

One of the differences between a home and a school is that there are fewer inhabitants. Limits in the home are easier to take because they are usually set by circumstances rather than by a person who is the all-powerful authority. Early in life a child learns that his world contains many limits. "It's *time* for school . . . for rest . . . for lunch . . . for bed . . . , etc." He learns an amazingly complex set of rules based on the notion that there is a proper time and place for just about everything.

Rules phrased as reminders: "It's not time for that yet," or "The bathroom or bedroom is the place for playing with yourself" are more readily accepted than a didactic "I told you not to start that now," or "Don't let me catch you doing that again." Thoughtless use of authority usually brings on a healthy fighting reaction from students. If you want a fight, this is a sure way to get one, but if you want to enforce a rule, it is better to offer a reminder for it in terms of place and time.

Because it is an *institution*, school is somewhat unreal or anti-human, although this is probably unnecessary. It seems to have been swept up in America's big-business syndrome, but it is naive and impractical to assume that competent individuals can be mass-produced by attempts to inculcate the same piece of learning in every youngster in the same room during the same day. Schools will never be efficient in the same way as a manufacturing plant simply because they work with and profit from those marvelous, if sometime irritating, individual human differences. We are not working for perfect sameness.

LEARNING

We have learned much about the world we live in and quite a bit about ourselves, but still know very little about *how* we learn. God knows we have run enough rats through mazes and tortured enough generations of college students with various learning experiments to find out a good deal about how rats acquire new skills and how and why college students participate in experiments, but we are still a long way from knowing how or why people learn. Much of the speculation offered by psychologists and educators is helpful to the teacher in viewing Johnny and Jane from a slightly different angle as learning animals. We should be honest with ourselves, however, and remember that it's merely speculation.

Most of us who work in education have read enough theories and research reports and done enough first-hand observing to formulate our own guesses as to how people learn, and we have altered our individual teaching styles accordingly. Don says: "I started my college teaching career with gracefully constructed and laboriously outlined lectures. As I got to know the students better and recalled my own college learning, my formal lectures gave way to rambling lecture-discussions whose loose outline was hidden from the students unless they took notes and tried to reconstruct the whole. With still more soul-searching and continued attempts to know my students, I no longer pretended to be lecturing but started meeting with student groups for an honest interchange that I believe stimulates learning. I still fret, with my students, about the course description in the school catalogue, and no one course tends to focus more than another on one area of the curriculum, but obsessive outlines are gone forever. I feel sure that few students are stimulated to learn from the passive experience endured during one of my lectures. Occasionally a gifted lecturer stirs the blood, makes a few points that can be remembered, and generally gets his listeners excited about his topic, but he is a rare bird. My own early lectures were designed to lure the student into swallowing some of my knowledge and regurgitating it later on an exam. I now try to poke around with questions and share my beliefs as Socrates did, because stirring up students to think seems to be the best way to provoke them to learn.

"But I may be making a mistake common to learning theories— generalizing about how people learn— whereas the individuals with whom I work have a variety of learning styles. Perhaps I'm still trying to find my optimal teaching style so that I can be as effective as possible in my profession. I know, however, that it will fit nicely with the learning styles of some students but not of others. Like all teachers, I cannot meet the learning needs of all students. This does not mean that one teacher's style is better or worse; it's simply different. I hope to attract those students who can make good use of *me*, while encouraging the others to use books and films and seek instructors whose style meets their own learning style.

"Learning is taking place before your very eyes, though it is hard to believe, since it is happening so conveniently at this point in the book. There is nothing in the preceding paragraphs that was not known to some part of me long before I set down the words today. Yet, as I was writing, several thoughts converged in the preceding paragraph and I saw that I had kidded myself by believing I could seek one teaching style that would help everyone learn best. Then came an example of what some learning theorists refer to as insight. My ruminations converged at one point in time and space and I realized that I have been toiling on the wrong end of the problem: on teaching rather than learning. I was trying to perfect *myself* as a universal *teacher* instead of figuring out how a teacher can best stimulate various styles of learning.

"There is little doubt of the existence of very different individual styles of learning. Whatever part intellect plays in the process, information must first be fed to us through our senses. And over the years, each of us has learned to favor one or more of them. We are more aware of absorbing sensory information through sight, hearing, touch, smell or taste than through body movement. Children tend to be more action-oriented than adults, and some of them have a special need to move about in space. To make such a child sit still for long periods of time is as cruel a torture as blocking another person's most useful sense by a blindfold, ear plugs, gloves, gas mask, or gag when he is trying his best to learn something in a new situation."

Asya says: "When starting to learn English at the age of 38, I found the best method was to type out new words so I could *see* them. I'm visual-minded (and a motor type, too) but absorb poorly through my ears. Teachers are becoming increasingly flexible in catering to individual styles of learning. A geography lesson is sometimes taught with children hopping from one 'continent' to another chalked on the floor; smell and taste are sometimes used for an entire chemistry lesson. Still the Victorian notion that youngsters learn best when seated in neat rows facing the blackboard continues to live on and haunt us.

"Emotions or feelings are also involved in learning. We mentioned feelings like pride and satisfaction earlier, but envy, humiliation, anger, sorrow, and joy also enter in. Before a teacher or student can plan to make the best use of feelings in learning, he must explore them. We so actively discourage expression of most feelings in our culture that often we must fish around for the proper words. This activity may at first seem extracurricular and a waste of time, but one clue to its value is the students' interest in it. What am I feeling? Is it anger, loathing, jealousy, hurt or something else? How is what I am feeling connected to my behavior of the past five minutes? It may turn out that one student, when jealous or angry, rapidly and precisely takes in and classifies information, but when hurt or repulsed, simply blocks the entry so that no information can get in.

"Self-understanding is not a bad goal in itself. The student who feels hurt may have found out that he should work with that feeling, giving up all pretense of school learning for the time being, since it won't 'take' anyhow. If he becomes angry in the middle of a lesson, however, he may be able to deal with that emotion later because it does not hinder his ability to assimilate new information."

ROLE OF FEELINGS IN LEARNING

This is an oversimplification, but the general idea is that feelings are related to learning, and only when we know more about them can we cope with them in a learning context. A teacher, as the central member of the class, can demonstrate how to identify and show feelings. A middle-aged wife and mother recently went back to school and became a teacher. During her first year she worried about how often she yelled at some of her second-graders—for instance, Gregory, who was usually out of his seat and loudly involved with a classmate when there was a need for relative quiet. One day she asked him to pass the wastebasket, then became involved in a problem with several other children. Catching sight of him out of the corner of her eye, she said sharply, "Gregory, get back to your seat this instant!" He returned to his seat but said plaintively, "You told me to pass the wastebasket." Her face registered dismay. "I'm terribly sorry, Gregory," she said, "I apologize. I got so involved with Susan and Geraldine that I forgot. You must be furious at me!" The boy smiled and said, "I like you because when you do something wrong, you say you're sorry."

Some interesting things happened in those few moments. The teacher owned up to some of her own feelings and Gregory owned up to some of his. It is not difficult to believe this honesty will affect the teacher-student relationship which will, in turn, affect Gregory's receptiveness to school learning.

When we were students, work was considered a virtue in and of itself. A popular distortion of the ideas behind progressive education persuaded some teachers for a few decades that fun was a virtue in and of itself. We now feel that satisfaction from a job well done or from something learned is the most pertinent educational reward. The work that usually goes hand-in-hand with learning is not always fun but it doesn't have to be unpleasant either. Work should be as enjoyable as possible, and there is usually more than one way to do it.

LEARNING NEEDN'T BE PAINFUL

A teacher depends upon feedback from the students to find out more interesting or bearable ways of approaching and completing a task, since one man's pleasure is another man's tedium. We believe that students should be encouraged to take the most scenic route to their destination instead of harboring the foolish idea that suffering will result in better learning. As teachers, we hope to see our students standing a little taller when they leave us because of the pride and satisfaction that can accompany growth.

The habitual and needless suffering that too often accompanies learning in today's schools reminds us that in more ways than one schools are not unlike prisons. The "inmates" are often told to sit, to stand, and to move about. Schools do not have to be that way, but in our culture schools and prisons have developed an amazingly similar philosophy about managing a large group of people who are not necessarily there by personal choice. They are also in uncomfortable agreement about how to teach and change the individual. It is high time for us to start thinking about school as something quite different from prison, though prisons would no doubt profit from adopting the features of a good school.

The essence of education is enjoying the freedom of being yourself after first finding out who you are. We cannot begin to predict what kind of world today's children will live in as adults, but certainly it is changing at a faster and faster rate. Tomorrow's citizens may well have to learn new occupations at least several times because old skills and knowledge will quickly become inadequate. The best we can do as educators is to encourage students to do their own learning, so they will not have to depend solely upon teachers. If the accent is placed on *how* to learn and *why* one may wish to learn this or that, we may help them find out about themselves and the world they live in. With a little more support, they may find the strength to *be* the persons they discover they are.

2

The Classroom as a Human Community

The classroom's very reason for existence is *learning*. We teachers can shape much of this learning, but we cannot fully control how and when it takes place, nor can we determine its particular form and flavor for the individual student when we are working with a group. Have you ever asked yourself (except in moments of despair) why we still put children into groups for learning? To be sure, it is less expensive than educating them individually but, more importantly, group interaction fosters a special kind of learning. Students learn a great deal from one another; the teacher is an expert in coordinating and facilitating learning that will help each child grow to adulthood able to master the problems peculiar to his environment. With twenty children and one professional, each child has multiple opportunities for intellectual and emotional stimulation. A student is often tuned to the same wavelength as his peers. A teacher may explain something over and over again, but many a youngster catches on only when it is interpreted in the seemingly casual language of a peer.

COMMUNITY

In the twentieth century almost all people live in communities, and a hermit is likely to be even more rare in the twenty-first century. Any skills or wisdom accumulated in school will be of use only within the framework of the community. The learning group thus becomes a necessity, not just an asset. It is worthwhile for students to assist in and stimulate each others' learning, but imperative for them to provide the model of the community where it will be put to use. This is an effective argument for public rather than private education, and against homogeneous grouping in schools. The more diverse the students, the more closely the group resembles the community outside, and the better the educational framework provided.

The class is by nature a community. Each of the many different kinds of communities in the world has various subgroups and leaders. The teacher, the most obvious leader of the total classroom community, influences it significantly. Most teachers in the United States consider themselves democratic rather than autocratic or *laissez-faire* leaders, yet they are a mixture of all three styles with one dominating. The extent to which your own professional behavior is autocratic or *laissez-faire* is worth thinking about, checking and rechecking.

A teacher whose style is predominantly democratic tends to structure a democratic classroom community which facilitates learning that will be useful in a democratic world. Almost all teachers favor democratic principles, at least intellectually. They consider autocratic methods "bad," but in a real classroom situation their respect for democracy is questionable. For example, a teacher whose overpermissiveness leads to disruption of the whole class and eventual anarchy has perhaps unconsciously encouraged this self-defeating set-up to justify seizing control. Sometimes there is an intermediary step; when violence or anarchy disrupts a classroom, the power usually falls into the hands of a student-leader who has neither the knowledge, strength, nor authority to restore democracy. Again the teacher grabs the power on the grounds that other methods have failed to preserve an effective working atmosphere. We two are not foolish enough or blind enough to pretend that the present world is democratic, but we are optimistic enough to believe that if we play our educational cards right, future generations will live in such a world.

A democratic leader, whether a mayor, senator, president, or teacher, cannot possibly meet the needs of all individuals in his community, control their impulses, or even be *aware* of all their needs and impulses. But a democratic leader can listen to the subgroups within his community and encourage the individuals to voice their feelings, thus providing satisfaction that may lead to better impulse control. A subgroup that has difficulty meeting this obligation to one or more members should yell loudly and the leader should listen.

A teacher or political aspirant cannot afford to overlook opportunities to reach and understand the individuals in the community who make up the subgroups and, in turn, the total group. The cook must know the effect of various ingredients on the final dish he prepares because each can make a profound difference. The teacher cannot always provide a hand, a lap, or an ear whenever it is needed, but someone else in the small classroom community can undoubtedly fill the bill at a given moment.

Actually the teacher plays many roles in the classroom: coordinator, orchestra conductor, stage director, authority, democratic leader, listener, guide, rephraser of questions (to make them easier to answer), devil's advocate, and voice of reality. Small wonder that teachers are so tired at the end of the day! One of the first of the teacher's many jobs in any classroom-community is to help students focus on their goals. There is no reason why everyone in a classroom-community cannot help to set the major learning goals for the year (the Board of Education, local newspaper editorials, parent pressure groups, assistant principal, and little-old-lady-next door to the contrary notwithstanding).

As coordinator with some previous experience in the school-learning game, the teacher can act as a resource. He can point out that many outside people *care* what kind of learning takes place there; that the Board of Education, the parents, the principal, and numerous others passionately believe that a particular kind of learning *should* go on. They care about children's education because the future of the neighborhood and of the world depends on it. Each has some reasons for believing in his particular kind of learning, and citizens of the class will find it worthwhile to consider these reasons seriously.

Your school system may have rigid requirements regarding what each student should cover during each year. If so, the students had better take this into account even if they do not make it their paramount consideration. The brave democratic teacher will admit that students can ignore the wishes of others about "proper" education but it is also the teacher's duty to stress the likely consequences of such revolutionary behavior in ways that help the students to realize the responsibility they are undertaking. No one can be *forced* to learn unless prodded by strong fear, and any learning then resulting is not likely to be useful.

Something is to be said for the brave democratic teacher whose students decide to rebel against the system. While facing the educational issues, this class approach ignores such personal factors as possible loss of the teacher's job. It is admittedly difficult for each of us to have the courage of our convictions, and the tests usually pester us throughout our adult lives. During such times the young-sters watch the teacher like hawks to see if he is an adult model they can trust, look up to, respect, and emulate. Imagine what can be learned from a teacher who is willing to put his job on the line for something he believes to be worthwhile!

You may be thinking, "Thanks a lot! That's all I need—to cope with the problem of helping the students set goals! It would take at least half the school year to get under way and I'd probably be fired before that." It may sound like a cop-out but we believe each teacher must walk his own path to what is traditionally called aca-demic freedom. You may disagree, but we sincerely hope you will try to see our point of view before deciding that we are wrong and, if so, in what way.

It is often easier to function as an authoritarian teacher who does not see the class as a community; he tells the youngsters what to learn, how to learn it, and when. We believe students learn in such a situation, but their time and energy are not being used optimally. Perhaps there is some sensible compromise between lofty ideals and that unpleasant earthbound monster, *reality*. We are painfully aware of the demands of reality, and feel that changes can be effected only by responsible people and for good reasons.

In addition to putting their heads together to set goals, the mem-bers of a classroom community should help set the rules for living together. A teacher who decides that everyone is to say "please," "thank you," and "you're welcome," will succeed with this cam-paign only if the students agree that it is desirable, for they will help to remind each other and enforce the rule. We are not talking about the abysmal pseudo-involvements too often encountered in a classroom discussion where the teacher says, "Why is it a good idea to say 'please' and 'thank you,' does anyone know? Raise your hand if you have some idea." After twenty minutes of this game with some of the veterans supplying the expected answers, a naive teacher may say, "We all agree now that it's a good idea to say 'please' and 'thank you' and must try to remind one another." It is a silly game at best; it would be more honest and save time and energies for the teacher to say, "I want every one of you to say 'please' and 'thank you' when appropriate and expect you to help me see that this order is carried out." At least the authoritarian tone is not hidden in a barrage of democratic language.

Since children can adjust to an authoritarian atmosphere more easily than adults, a teacher who gives honest and straight directives may soon build a class that works with him harmoniously. There is no reason why adaptable adjustable children cannot learn to follow orders. They can! But when they are adults they may look around for someone to tell them what to do.

If a more democratically oriented teacher believes that "please" and "thank you" are important tools there is no reason why he cannot say so. He might even explain *why* he holds a brief for polite language. The other citizens will then know where he stands. If he is respected and sincerely practices what he preaches, the polite-speech contagion may well spread.

You have undoubtedly noticed that when a teacher is sincerely polite and considerate with his students they usually try their best to return the compliment. But if he uses "please" as a sarcastic reminder of his private rule, he can forget the whole campaign. His sweet words will be returned with sincerity only when the students are ready, willing, and able to comply.

Police tactics are largely a waste of time. A teacher cannot depart from his coordinating and other duties often enough for effective policing of each student's activities. Most of the control, as in any community, must come from within the individual himself and from group pressure. If the group has worked hard to fashion sensible rules, infractions will not be taken kindly. Only an unusual person can consistently buck the pressure of his peers.

When the students' self control and group control fail, it is certainly sensible for the teacher to apply the brake and assume the role of community policeman momentarily. But he should give some thought to helping both the individual involved and the group itself guard against future loss of control. Otherwise the teacher will have his foot on the brake more often than on the accelerator, and no one will get very far. In this situation, knowledge of the make-up of classroom subgroups and skill in handling class discussion will be very useful to the teacher.

GROUPS

The first step in getting to know your students is to view them individually, and the second step is to view them as a group. Actually, you must work with them as a group from the first moment school opens each year. Mobs are terrifying, but groups are reassuring. The difference between a mob and a group is primarily one of organization.

A mob frightens us because it is unpredictable; we do not know what holds it together or where it is heading. Each classroom is a group containing a variety of subgroups. With careful observation, the teacher can get to know the larger group with its subgroups, to predict what it will do in a given situation, to work with it.

Each student is bound to belong to several subgroups, and to have his special role in the larger class group. Subgroups form around issues and personal needs touched off by the wide variety of discussion topics, human interactions, and even the weather changes during a school day. A case in point is the split on authority orientation. Some youngsters generally do what the authority would wish whether he is present or not. We might call them the *pro-authority* subgroup. Others seem to fight authority in any form, including (or especially) the teacher. We might call them the *anti-authority* subgroup. Finally youngsters in the middle subgroup are *now pro-* and *now anti-authority*, depending on how the wind blows and which orientation is more attractive at the moment.

A seasoned teacher knows better than to take on the class in a battle; since he is vastly outnumbered the students are sure to come out on top. Instead of fighting back when his authority is challenged by the "anti" group, he can request that they state their dissatisfactions, objections, and disagreements more clearly. He must respect them and reward their efforts when they help the whole class to learn. With such a response they will eventually present the opposing point of view in an orderly fashion. A government cannot function well without such a balancing of subgroups.

When a force within a group leads to the formation of a subgroup, another subgroup forms representing the contrary force and a middle group consisting of those who vacillate between the two. The larger group naturally tries to maintain its stability. An attempt by the teacher to suppress one subgroup only creates an interesting war, a group imbalance in which recruits are sought from the middle subgroup. The teacher is left holding the bag, having fought most of the students and completely lost a war, that, like most wars, served the needs of a few people and should never have begun.

It is far more worthwhile for the teacher to use all that energy working with the subgroups for the benefit of the whole class. Let the opposing groups present their case on any issues and let each pupil learn how to weigh evidence and arguments and make up his own mind. Let the class learn how to accept opposing groups, each having enough room to work and live comfortably, rather than making a hard and fast "right" and "wrong" rule on every issue.

You learn a lot working with subgroups but a lot of "playing by ear" seems to be needed. Like the stage director or the choreographer, you must see the subgroups in action before trying to encourage constructive balance. And the process is endless. When one actor or dancer moves, a new *gestalt* is formed and a new balance of forces must be sought.

SOCIOGRAMS

Of course, it helps to know the make-up of each subgroup. Various sociogrammatic techniques for gathering the information have been developed by leaders in the field. You will find out about them by spending a few hours in the library. We have developed a very simple "x-ray" form that usually does the trick. The kind of subgroups revealed depends upon the leading questions posed.

Here is how we do it. If we want to know about friendship clusters, we ask students to pick the person they would like to sit next to on the school bus, stand next to when lined up for dismissal, or sit next to in class. Any such general question will do as long as no particular skills or talents are involved in the question. It is just another way of asking, "Who do you like?" without causing embarrassment. The question must be appropriate to the age group and type of class.

It is wise to caution them to work independently; for older students you might say that any responses meant to tease one another or show off will spoil a complicated thing you're trying to do and reduce their chances of getting their first choice. Of course, if your students have become open and receptive, you may simply say you want a picture of the class friendship groups so you can better work with them. In any event, you will sincerely do your best to honor their requests.

If you want to find out the subgroups aligned on other issues (*e.g.,* their feeling about going to school, in general), you might ask what person they would nominate for a committee to decide the length of the school day. Or, for natural work groups, you might ask what person they would like to work with on a project committee. As you can see, the question should elicit a response revealing the talent or issue you are investigating.

We strongly recommend that you keep the accumulated data to yourself. Showing them to the class would be playing with dynamite because of the great risk of someone getting hurt by having his lack of attractiveness made public. The few people not chosen are often heartily disliked (and disliking), or unnoticed, by the class. They undoubtedly need your help in establishing some relationship with their peers, but will feel hurt and betrayed if their plight is made clear to the others.

Once you have chosen the question, the instructions may go something like this:

"Please write the numbers one, two, and three on a piece of paper, leaving room between. Next to the number one, write the name of the person you would most like to work with on the committees to plan our year-end festival. Next to the number two, write the name of your second choice, and next to the number three, your third choice. Please don't discuss your answers or it will spoil the whole thing. Someone else might change his choice, and then I'd be less likely to arrange to give you yours. Also, calling out might hurt someone's feelings even if you'd be doing it only for fun. I'll do the best I can to give you your choice. When you've finished, please fold your papers and I'll collect them. I hope to have the committees set up by next Tuesday. If you aren't happy with your committee, stick with it for a while and then if it's really not working out we'll try to shift you."

It takes at least a couple of hours to go over the data for a class of twenty or thirty; the more time you spend, the more you learn. The time-consuming step, after the data have been collected, tabulated and mulled over, is to set up the committees, seating plan, or whatever else according to the results of the original question.

When the responses are all in, we suggest dividing a sheet of lined paper lengthwise into five columns. In the first column, write the names of all of the students in alphabetical order. The second column is for a code which will be explained later. The third, fourth, and fifth columns are for each student's first, second, and third choices. The names are entered just as they were written. The following illustration may help:

Name	Code	First Choice	Second Choice	Third Choice
Adams, Ben	0-2-1	Irv Gunn	Sally I.	Jean E.
Boman, Jean	4-1-0	Irv Gunn	Jeanne Evans	Sally Ingman
Carolli, Tom	0-0-0	Jeannie Bo	Mia Harris	Jean Evans
Davis, Al	1-0-0	Sally Jacobs	Benny	Jeanne E.
Evans, Jeanne	0-1-5	Jeannie B.	Irv Gunn	Ella Fort
Fort, Ella	0-0-1	Sally	Jean Boman	Irv Gunn
Gunn, Irving	3-2-2	J. Boman	Mia Harris	Ben Adams
Harris, Mia	0-2-0	Irv Gunn	Sal	Jean Evans
Ingman, Sally	1-2-1	Jean B.	Ben	Irv Gunn
Jacobs, Shelley	1-0-0	Al Davis	Irv Gunn	Jean E.

We will try to show how speculations or hypotheses can be based on these data, though it makes more sense and is much more fun when you know the real flesh-and-blood youngsters involved. Some hypotheses are immediately discarded because they simply don't fit the youngster as you know him. Others provide surprises; you watch the particular youngster to see if his behavior and actions support the hypothesis.

For example, when the ten youngsters (with fictional names) had written in their choices, we assigned each a code number of three digits representing the number of times he was selected as a first, second and third choice, respectively. We also circled any mutual choices, *e.g.*, Sally Ingman and Ben Adams listed each other, indicating some mutual attraction or respect.

Let us assume that the question was something simple like "Who would you like to sit with . . . ?" and we planned to seat the ten in two groups. What have we learned about the individuals? Was Tom Carolli not chosen by anyone because he is the only very poor boy in the class and wears cast-off clothes? Or do the others hardly notice him because he is so quiet? Al Davis and Shelley Jacobs at least have each other, or do they seek each other's company so the others won't notice they're so alone? Al wrote "Sally" instead of "Shelley." Although none too bright he surely knows the names have different spellings. Was it a slip of the pen? Shelley is somewhat feminine in mannerisms and Al works awfully hard at being the tough guy. Does the obvious difference pull them together?

Ella Fort always seems involved with the others and yet was chosen only once (Jeanne Evans' third choice). Could it be that when the chips are down, Ella, the only black student in the class, is socially excluded? Do the others really like her, or has she learned how to remain active and smiling and charming on the fringes, so that no one notices she is an outsider?

Jean Boman and Irv Gunn always seem very popular, but putting each other as first choice is somewhat surprising. One would have guessed they were in too keen competition to choose each other at all. Could it be that the apparent competition is a play, an attempt to attract? Jean and Irv, both socially successful, chose the same classmates who chose them, but Jeanne Evans, whose popularity is of lesser magnitude, chose only one person who chose her. Could it be that she is not very sensitive to who likes her and who doesn't, and that's the reason for her also-ran sort of popularity?

This is enough to know what kind of fruitful speculating is possible. The information, which makes subsequent classroom observation more useful and to-the-point, is mostly about individuals, however. As they are assigned to seating groups governed by their choices, you can see how they relate to each other in subgroups. The only way to grasp this aspect is to try to arrange groups according to the students' expressed wishes. The more time and energy you invest in the project, the more you will learn about subgroup relatedness. We would have assigned them like this (you are, of course, free to argue with us):

Group 1	Group 2
1. Ben Adams	1. Jean Boman
2. Al Davis	2. Tom Carolli
3. Ella Fort	3. Jeanne Evans
4. Sally Ingman	4. Irv Gunn
5. Shelley Jacobs	5. Mia Harris

A lot of research has been done on group psychodynamics to find what specific knowledge of group counseling and group therapy can be applied to group education. We believe classroom discussions can be divided into several categories. First, the teacher or another authority steers the discussion to a topic holding interest and importance for each youngster and for the total group, including the teacher himself. We call this theme-centered discussion; it can be related to sex, social science, current events, or any other topic of interest. Whatever the theme, the discussion becomes triangular, with one side representing the youngster, one the total group, and the third the theme. The leader must keep to the subject and skillfully steer youngsters back to it when they wander, by something like, "Johnny, I'm not sure I see how your comment is relevant to our topic today."

The second type of discussion is led by the group of students without an authority figure. In a good working group a student leader is bound to emerge; the teacher is considered a resource person to be called on only if needed. He doesn't even have to be in the same room but should be close enough to be summoned at a moment's notice.

A third type, which we call "group rap," is becoming more and more a part of the everyday curriculum. Both students and teacher(s) are present during this hour, and all of them really struggle to find acceptable solutions to the conflicts and problems encountered during the school day.

One reason most of us like bull sessions better than formal lessons is their very lack of structure. There is always the possibility of an adventure into the unknown, while in formal lessons, with the accent on structure, hard work can lead only to a foregone conclusion. The difference is between zeroing in on the answer and reaching out for new questions. In the kind of class discussion we recommend, students can eat their cake and have some of it too. They can reach out for new questions while working toward answers if you do not require the right answer today. In fact, you may never get the right answer, but will have to settle for answers that *seem* right until more evidence is uncovered. We believe this, in itself, is something worth learning: *There are no absolutely, permanently right answers in our human world; we must continue to seek new evidence, which will change our temporary answers.*

Group discussion includes: (1) the theme-centered type, (2) the spontaneous type inspired by some occurrence in the classroom or an outside happening (such as a birth or death in the family of a student); and (3) the regularly scheduled free discussion to which the students can bring complaints and conflicts that arise during their daily interaction. We think of this free discussion as an integral part of the curriculum. It can take place before academic subjects get under way or at the close of the school day. The idea is to air positive and negative feelings and reactions—the problems and conflicts of the classroom community. Each day is marked by unresolved questions, fights and complaints. The teacher may respond immediately with, "We can't go into that now; hold it for our discussion period. Meanwhile, let's go on with our work." The student feels that his problems are postponed rather than disregarded. He will have a chance to express his hurt or abused feelings. The teacher will not give pat answers—"You should (shouldn't) have done it" or "You were right (wrong)"—but will instead try to activate the group members to express their feelings about what is happening. You may be surprised at the results if you say, "Let's try to understand what actually happened" or "Jack and Dick, what made you start fighting? How did you feel before the blow-up?" The teacher should bear in mind that many manifestations of anger, hostility or fright may arise from prejudice, *e.g.*, against Jews, Catholics, Blacks, the poor, the rich, and so on. As soon as possible, such feelings should be brought out and handled with bluntness and sincerity.

"I visited a model school in Vienna for a number of weeks," Asya says. "It was run by two teachers, Drs. Ferdinand Bernbaum and Oscar Spiel, who regularly encouraged group discussions at the close of each school day. Among the topics were decisions for the next day or week and setting rules as well as means of enforcing them. I became convinced that the youngsters learned a great deal in that one hour about living together, their motivations and their behavior, and were gaining understanding of themselves and their classmates. They seemed to think and reason, to plan, to take active part in things, to be helpful and cooperative. They were developing more self-confidence, becoming more friendly and considerate. In short, I felt the group discussion contributed enormously to their character development and the growth process."

Such free discussions do not, of course, detract from the value of theme-centered discussions, whether on sex, prejudice, racial tensions, or any other subject suitable to the age group.

Free discussion groups are best chaired by students in rotation, with the teacher in the role of helpful assistant who actively enters the discussion on request unless intervention seems truly essential. It is especially important for junior high school students to assume the chairmanship because they need to feel that adults trust them. The teacher may convey such feelings by: "We believe you can learn to handle many situations adequately by yourselves, and can even help us with policies and with establishing or changing the rules and regulations we need to ensure a good atmosphere. As a group you can better help us to understand your needs and desires."

The theme-centered type of discussion is, of necessity, more structured. Adhering to the common topic contributes to the students' self-discipline and orderly thinking. Such themes as planning and evaluating a particular group activity, or a concerted effort for a common purpose, friendliness, and how to be a real friend—all can further more accurate thinking as well as help to correct distortions.

The overall goals for every classroom are to help the students be more productive, feel better, and achieve maximal growth. We can assume that these common aims can be used as a central theme. Each person in the group is the "I," their sum total is the "we," and the third element is the theme itself. Each side of the interactional triangle is equally important. If one "I" (student) is not involved with the "we" or the "theme," his side of the triangle is practically dead, throwing it out of balance and possibly precipitating a collapse. A weak or missing part of a triangle is like a chain with a missing link.

The role of any teacher or group leader is to restore the dynamic balance of the three sides of the triangle. When any "I" is disturbed and "not with it," when the group does not simultaneously participate in a theme, or abandons a set theme, the leader must restore the balance of the triangle.

Let us keep in mind that teachers should have respect for each individual, whether teacher or student, for the group interacting around the theme, and the communication and search involved in it. Only if each individual is respected as a body, a mind, a spiritual being with sensitivity and emotions, can the group command respect as an entity. This premise would ensure the best living-learning experience. The teaching and learning of a group is determined not only by the interactional triangle but also by the historical geographical environment in which the group meets. The group process takes place in a specific classroom community, not in a vacuum. The teacher who uses the theme-centered discussion method should try to be sensitive to what is going on today in his classroom.

Any class group, even one homogeneously formed according to certain factors, represents many different past experiences, interests and values. It is possible to learn a great deal from the diversity and disagreement within it. When you are faced with two good but opposing arguments on some point, you must think, "Which is right? Which person seems to be getting to the heart of it? Could they both be right? Is each one right about different parts of the question? Do they both sound wrong because the whole question rubs me the wrong way? That reminds me of something else neither of them has taken into consideration," and so on. Human beings have a penchant for organizing and bringing order out of chaos. Opposing points of view represent a conflict to be resolved. A person is strongly stimulated to begin thinking if the issue interests him.

"The learning potential from diversity and disagreement has caused me to think seriously about the kind of education I would like for my own children," says Don.

"I know that some private schools offer an educational format vastly superior to that found in the usual public school system, but the families who are interested and can afford to send children there represent an unnaturally homogeneous group. My children can find far more diversified background experiences and current values in any public school, but it will be unlikely to tap more than a fraction of that diversity during the formal school hours. This is a dilemma. The public schools have the raw material, and some of the private schools have the know-how to use it successfully. I am sticking with public schools until my children are old enough to consult, while eagerly sniffing the winds for signs of change in the style of learning made available in the public schools."

This is probably a good place to admit that the class discussions we recommend *do* leave less time for formal lessons. In fact, if youngsters are introduced to such discussions after years of traditional curriculum, it seems doubtful that they can go back to anything remotely resembling it. The excitement tends to level off after the students get used to their new freedom, however, for many reasons. First, it represents an ever-present responsibility for each participant. He is constantly engaged in the learning process. The resulting interaction keeps him involved with the other students as well as with the material to be explored and mastered. Students eventually want a rest from it. Also, one cannot learn enough about the history of the world, mathematics, chemistry, or spelling from open discussions alone. We expect the students will become sufficiently motivated to go to libraries and lecture halls with a new appetite for knowledge. We believe that without open discussion there is little genuine learning, even though the teacher tries his best to transmit the prepared lesson. Covertly, student attention is usually somewhere else. The static and passive elements of this situation (in which the student is captive) promote unrest. "Let's rattle the teacher," they may think, "and make this prison time more interesting." Certainly there is little to lose and much to gain from open class discussions.

A teacher considering the hoped-for gains from a year's experience with group discussion in his class should be ready to have his own goals tempered by his students' past experiences and current goals. The beginning of the school year is a good time to take a careful look at your students and the school in which they have functioned up to now. Anything you can learn about the community they live in will help. An atmosphere foreign to you demands exploring. The child-rearing customs, the peer codes of communication, recreational activities, typical values and styles of nonverbal communication, religious beliefs and practices, even the kinds of food eaten, are essential to your understanding of how these youngsters cope with their particular world. A week spent walking the streets and chatting with parents and merchants can pay royal dividends. The year must somehow represent a blend of where you and your students are "at."

If the students' previous school experience has been autocratic, the structure early in the year will have to be more rigid than seems proper to a democratically oriented teacher. Conversely, if their previous teacher had an inept "hands off" or "do-as-you-please" policy, a teacher will have to bear with the false "freedom" while introducing structure and rules gradually so that students do not become inhibited and/or docile.

Progress toward goals acceptable to both teacher and students usually seems slow. Most groups never reach their goals, but they are closer to them by the end of the school year. Once a teacher has a feeling for his students, he can set reasonable private goals that will lesson the risk of his getting an ulcer. He may work toward a two-minute open discussion for democratic decision-making by the third week of school and hope for a four-minute period by the fourth week, seven minutes by the fifth week, twelve minutes by the sixth, and up to a full class period by the end of the school year. There will be ups and downs, as with any kind of human growth, but most teachers get used to that rather quickly anyway.

The question of when to have discussions is a good one. An exasperated young teacher recently said, "I tried to suggest that we discuss our noise problem but no one could hear me!" At the same meeting another teacher said, "What do you do when one child just starts hitting another? I would feel simple-minded turning to the class and saying, 'What do the rest of you think about this?'"

Both of these teachers are talking about a good technique applied at the wrong moment. An emergency has to be dealt with promptly. If someone is getting hurt and the class has failed to control the episode, the teacher obviously must act as a policeman until the emergency is past. A noise level that threatens to bring down the wrath of neighboring teachers and the assistant principal has to be reduced or the whole community may suffer.

The time for discussion is when the heat of the emergency is past. The teacher can then say, "We have a problem and must try to solve it. This doesn't mean that I am going to listen to your suggestions and tell you which ones I think are right. It means that after talking over reasons for doing on thing or another, we will all have to agree on some solution to the problem even if it turns out to be wrong later." The language is adapted to the age and background of the students involved but the underlying "we" message remains. The teacher is promising help and guidance but demanding that the students rightfully assume responsibility for themselves as a community.

It takes time for a group to get the hang of taking full responsibility for itself as a community. One of the most difficult tasks for the teacher is to try to predict how much or how little responsibility the class community can take at any given moment. You will probably go too far one way, correct yourself, then go too far the other way. It is something like driving a car on a road that has subtle curves. Following the road takes you someplace, providing you are careful to alter your steering to follow the curves. If too much responsibility is placed on students all at once, they may find it a burden and throw it off altogether; conversely, too little responsibility stunts their growth. Very careful listening to the feedback information they offer will give you a reading of their comfort level in respect to the responsibility you would like them to assume, and feel they can.

You can continue to convey, in words and by your behavior, that you are ready to give sympathy and comfort and even take over now and then, but as much of the responsibility as possible should be placed right on the students' collective shoulders, where it belongs.

Students are accustomed to hearing such words as "should," "shouldn't," "good," "bad," "do," and "don't" from teachers and parents. As you listen to student discussions and see them about to assume a certain responsibility you often think, "Oh, dear, they're so young. That's not a very good idea. There's a better way to do it." We have found it better to let them do it their own way ("Please, Mother, I'd rather do it myself!"). After they've had a lot of experience with you in the role of a more experienced bystander instead of a god or an authority, you can begin to add your two cents' worth to the discussion. If you try too early, however, they'll follow or disregard your advice (as with the advice of previous authorities), though you intended only to share your thoughts and not issue orders. Before you even suggest that they consider or do something else, ask yourself if going on their merry way without your "wisdom" will bring disaster. Once in a while, when you have stayed out of it, you'll find they were doing just fine—a chastening experience!

We don't mean to come on "holier than thou." Sometimes we fail to follow our own convictions in teaching or other work with youngsters, but we would like to offer a good rule of thumb: *Swallow your advice unless catastrophe seems imminent.* If you follow this rule even fairly well, the students will eventually ask for your opinion, consider it, then accept or reject it. And don't take rejection personally—you will be heard, but not until asked.

The three basic rules in the "how-to" of leading discussions are: (1) listen, (2) clarify, and (3) summarize. The first means you really listen. Most of us listen selectively, we hear what we want to hear because we easily agree or disagree with it. It takes time to develop the skill of careful listening, but once you have done so, it is hard to get away from all the people who want to talk to you. We all like to be heard and understood, and seek out people who really listen.

The second rule means that when you are not sure what someone is saying you should ask a clarifying question or encourage such questions from other members in the group. You cannot tell him anything without violating the first rule, but you can say, "I don't understand," or "I'm not sure what you mean by . . . " In this way you will help the speaker and the other listeners to clarify the points in question. Don't be sneaky and use such questions to preach or lecture (*e.g.*, "Do you mean to say you believe it is right to . . . ?" or "I can't understand how any healthy young American could mean what you seem to be saying"). If you start that kind of game you can kiss genuine discussion goodbye.

The third rule means that you try to be the historian for the discussion (if someone else doesn't take over), keeping the main factors in focus and letting individuals work toward their own conclusions ("So far we've found that some people in the group believe the war is justified because it will save American lives, others believe it is not justified because Americans and others are being killed, while still others believe war is never justified"). At this point you may have to swallow an impulse to steer the course of the discussion or insert your own opinion, directly or indirectly. As soon as you ally yourself with one side or the other or try to direct the discussion, you lose the role of impartial facilitator. Your participation will be welcome only after the group has learned to hold discussions without a leader; you'll know if and when the happy day arrives because the students will begin to demand to know what you think.

These three rules help the teacher shed more light on the discussion without being judgmental. Everyone can better follow the course of the discussion because of the leader or facilitator, yet no one feels put down. Each voice is equally worthwhile and commands equal respect.

Discussions often are disappointing at first, especially if the children are young. When trying to deal with some trouble in the classroom, they may offer every punitive solution they ever have heard of, plus a few horrors of their own creation. They may recommend that the next person who starts a fight be sent to the principal, sent home, made to stand in the corner, or even be thrown out of the window. If these punishments are offered seriously they must be considered seriously and the community must try to foresee the consequences of invoking them. Frivolous suggestions do not need any more recognition than a smile. Beware though; at times it's hard to tell when someone is kidding. A child may make a suggestion with a smile because he is afraid of being ridiculed, though he is dead serious. You may have to check with him, controlling your voice tone to avoid implying that he couldn't possibly be serious. You may feel somewhat self-conscious doing this at first, lest you sound naive or stupid, but the students will eventually perceive your attitude as respectful caution rather than stupidity.

We would like to give a few examples of how profitable discussions can blossom during the school day. The class may decide that since the discussions frequently carry them off on tangents, time should be reserved for them at the end of the period or the day. But more often than not you'll have to strike while the iron is hot. For example, you may be in the middle of a natural science lesson when a student says, "Why does the book always make it look like there's only one way to figure out how high a building is or what the air pressure is?"

"They don't want to confuse you," says another student, provoking a few giggles.

"I can't read that book anyway. I fall asleep every time I try, man," says a boy in the back row.

A pretty long-haired girl sitting near the window says, "I'd rather learn to appreciate the feeling of sunlight on my face than to figure out how it gets to me from the sun."

The teacher might say something like: "It sounds as if some of you don't care for the book and some of you don't care for the subject. Shall we talk about it now or would you rather wait until we get to the end of this period?"

If the experience is new, they will all jump at the chance for the discussion but if they are accustomed to this approach a sizable number may say, "Let's wait." To save endless and unprofitable discussion, the teacher usually makes a decision based on what seems to be the dominant need of the group or he may ask for a show of hands. Many factors have to be considered: If much ground will be lost by interrupting the lesson and if only 30 per cent of the students want to start the discussion, it is probably a good idea to postpone it. The reasons can be stated briefly and the lesson continued with the promise of picking up the discussion at some later time.

To cite another example, a class may be discussing *Lord of the Flies* when a boy says, "I don't know why, but I felt kind of scared the whole time I was reading the book."

The boy in the seat behind gives him a playful punch and says, "Man, that's 'cause you're scared all the time anyway."

A wave of laughter conveys to the teacher's sensitive ear that there is a considerable amount of tension in the group.

A girl in a front seat says softly, "I felt kind of embarrassed sometimes. It wasn't like reading a school book." She blushes.

A hearty male yells out, "Let's all get shipwrecked on an island and do our thing! Only we'll have chicks!"

The teacher tunes his ear. What are they saying? Is this a discussion?

Another girl says, "My mother says it isn't good to read books like that because it puts ideas into your head like bad television shows."

"Try reading *Portnoy's Complaint!*" comes from a scholarly boy with thick glasses who almost never speaks out.

The teacher says, "Are you just having fun or should we have a discussion about the kinds of feelings you got when you read *Lord of the Flies* and other books? If you're just horsing around I'd like to get on, but if you're serious let's talk about it."

"Some books I don't like to read because they make me feel kind of sad," a girl says.

And so the discussion gets under way, and the teacher tries to help the students focus on what they want to talk about. It may turn out to be a need to share feelings not often shared honestly. It may turn out to be an attempt to differentiate worthwhile books from those that are a waste of time. There is no way to predict the course of the discussion but it is bound to go into areas that interest the students.

In an upper elementary grade in the middle of a math lesson, for no apparent reason a boy may yell out, "Well, your mother sucks!" A book is thrown and chaos looms. You quell the emergency and say, "What's going on here, anyway?"

"Tommy's got a filthy mouth," Georgia volunteers.

"Juan's all the time picking on him," Maria says.

"I wish they'd quit messing up my learning," Ethel says. "How we ever going to get to be somebody?"

"Tommy's a nigger," Juan says quietly.

Chaos is again imminent. The teacher says, "Look! I'm not sure what gives but at least two people are having trouble with each other and it's cutting into our learning time. Maybe we should take time out to try to help them settle it and to figure out how we can keep such arguments from starting. What do you think?"

"Can't do nothing with Juan 'cause he's a dumb honkey," says Miriam.

"That's what makes people fight, when you call them something like that," says Anthony.

"It can even make you mad if somebody calls you a Negro," says Melissa. "I always tell them I'm *Black*, not Negro."

"You can call me anything you want long's you don't mess with me," says Georgia.

"People cuss at people or just call 'em names 'cause they're mad, but sometimes they ain't mad at the guy they're calling names," Anthony says distractedly while looking out the window.

"It sounds as if it's the *feeling behind* the name you're called that makes you feel like fighting," the teacher says.

The discussion is under way. It may not solve the problem today but everyone will start thinking about it.

In a lower elementary grade, a child may say, "My grandfather died last night."

"My grandfather died, too," says another.

"Well, mine is going to die," says a little boy not about to be left out.

"We had a guinea pig that died," Carol adds. "His name was Happy and he's in heaven now."

"That's where my grandfather is."

"That's where President Kennedy is," adds another, surprisingly introducing history to the discussion.

"Him and Martin Luther King got shot and Robert Kennedy too. They got killed," says another historian.

"I'm not going to die until I get all grown up and get married and have children and live a long, long time," says Virgil but somehow you hear a question mark at the end of his assertion.

"Sometimes kids get run over and then they're dead," says Pete, and a relative quiet descends on the class.

"I bet it hurts to be dead," says Sally.

There is no need for the teacher to enter this discussion just yet. The children are hearing one another; they are busy thinking, contributing, and interacting. A little later the teacher may want to summarize their collective feeling on the subject: "It sounds as if many of you think dying or being dead is pretty scary." You can see what will come next. Spontaneous classroom discussions sometimes get on quite nicely without any intervention.

If a teacher does not "use" discussion to lead students to some point, they will very likely use it to lead themselves to new questions. The teacher can serve best by clarifying and by resisting the temptation to direct. The students' new questions demand new searching for new answers—the royal road to learning.

LIVING

Children are required by law to attend school. Our nation feels so strongly about educational opportunity that school is a "must." The only sane reason for this is that learning will hopefully help us achieve a more satisfying life.

We spend our lives in communities made up of groups, and the class group offers a good mini-community that can prepare us for living in the adult world. If we want individually responsible citizens who can create a democratic world, we must help children to grow in that direction. Each person in the class community is a citizen, but the teacher is paid to live in it by the larger community, because he is a citizen with special responsibilities.

As teachers, we must help students solve problems in ways that will enable them to solve future, unforseen problems. The task becomes increasingly ticklish as our world changes more and more rapidly, making it increasingly harder to predict even the types of problems which tomorrow's adults will encounter. Because the teacher has usually had more, and more varied, living experiences than his students, he is expected to know how to cope with diverse situations. Whether he has learned the necessary techniques through his own schooling or through living, they must work when used with students.

Conscious use of what psychologists call *reinforcement* can be very helpful, *e.g.*, finding out what the students consider genuine rewards, and using them immediately following behavior you hope to encourage, or withholding them following behavior you hope to see less often. It is worth remembering, however, that the teacher's hysterical screaming at an offender or a subgroup may prove to be an attractive reward. You cannot take for granted any reinforcement or reward until you have good evidence. The common assumption that a smile or a pat on the back is an unfailing reward may not be true. A smile to a student from the wrong teacher can be the kiss of death if his peers are watching.

A few golden rules almost never fail. A lawyer friend of ours decided to take a course in child psychology to help him cope with his newborn daughter some years ago. He remembers little about the course except that *substitution* is a good idea: If you take something away from a youngster offer him an equally attractive substitute. The rule has stood him in good stead with his children, his grandchildren, and several generations of children of friends for whom he has been a kind of Pied Piper. It works like magic in the classroom, too.

A teacher-friend recently told an anecdote about Jésus, a usually able math student who seemed bored one day during a lesson on this subject. He was seeking the attention of nearby students with a display of muscles and masculine wit. The teacher, who knew better than to take away the adulation and attention without offering something in return, said, "Jésus, will you please give me a hand? I'll take this side of the room and you take the other. Anyone having trouble with the assignment can request individual help at his own desk until he catches on."

The integrity and responsibility of the individual and the group must not be violated. We are not suggesting that you play tricks on students or manipulate them in a condescending manner. Full respect for the worth of each individual is central to our orientation. In talking about such techniques as reinforcement or substitution, we recommend that the teacher try to be *aware* of the ways in which he is attempting to alter the students' behavior. Most of us continuously attempt to alter the behavior of almost every meaningful person in our lives but we are not usually aware of this fact. We use a storehouse of techniques assembled before we had much facility with language or knew what they were called. We should try to track down the basis for our motivation to alter behavior. Are we trying to please ourselves? Or are we convinced that the alteration is essential to the students' growth?

We hope the teacher can become tolerant enough to let others (including his students) be the people they are and want to be. We hope the teacher can be available to facilitate change when a student asks for help, without playing God and deciding who should change and in what way. We also hope the teacher will become increasingly aware of techniques with which he tries to promote change, and admit to himself and his students that he is using them. As he becomes able to let the other person be, such techniques will no longer be needed, and that will be the end of the problem. But until such a fine day, let us work for awareness of and honesty in the ways in which we influence others.

When people live together closely, emergencies arise in the course of the day. The fact that you are trying to build a model community together and everyone in the class-community is learning to assume citizen responsibility, individually and collectively, will lead to resolution of many of the conflicts underlying the emergencies. Many but not all of the emergencies will be prevented. An alert, sensitive teacher can also head off many emergencies before they become acute.

The rumble of human thunder is heard before a storm strikes the classroom in the form of a temper tantrum or a fist fight. In this short interval something can often be done to prevent the storm. A remark something like "I told you to stay in your seat, now I'm warning you" from the teacher heightens the tension. Each dramatic step leads to another. The teacher's message is that he has heard the thunder. Unsure of how to handle the problem of control, he inadvisedly refers it back to the student whose signal already shows that his own controls are coming unglued. If they were in good shape, he would have stayed in his seat in the first place and there would have been no rumblings.

If the teacher can recognize the thunder as a warning of the youngster's need to borrow control for a moment, he might say something like "Cynthia, come up here a moment. There's something I want to show you." When the child arrives at the teacher's side, a friendly arm around the shoulder or mere physical proximity to the "authority" may reduce the tension enough to permit the lesson to continue. If blackboard work is involved, the teacher might show Cynthia an easy shortcut in arithmetic. Or Cynthia may act as an assistant or secretary, writing on the board as the teacher talks. The thunder has been heard, the control has been borrowed, the storm has passed over.

When you hear thunder and don't know how to lend control yourself, call on the rest of the community. For example, "It looks as if Cynthia and I are headed for trouble and I don't know how to prevent it. Any ideas from the rest of you?" Actually, merely designating the class community as the control agent may lend Cynthia enough strength to tide her over.

Emergencies, like other kinds of lessons, can be handled in ways that do not undermine the individual's or the group's responsibility. As adult in charge, you need to lend strength or controls, but keep in mind that this is only an emergency crutch. Each student has to stand on his own feet, psychologically speaking. The community must function as a healthy autonomous organism. It is fine for the teacher to become a crutch when needed, but an unhealthy dependency results if the person or community is not encouraged to do without the crutch as soon as possible, and if an individual or a community can function *only* if you are there, the situation is bad indeed.

We have so strongly emphasized the community in this book that you may think we have no use for solitude or privacy. Not so! In our opinion, the integration and growth that go hand-in-hand with learning are largely private matters. Each person must have a time and a place to be with himself—something virtually ignored in twentieth-century America. The last few decades have seen increasing interest in the forms of meditation, perhaps an expression of our desire to be alone without being lonely. We need to find ways to be productive and to satisfy aloneness. We would strongly urge any community, including a classroom community, to seek both physical and psychological privacy.

Private communication is hard to come by in the classroom; we recommend that the community arrange a place for it—a whispering corner, a broom closet, or even a stairwell. There should be a place where two people, especially a teacher and child, can be together without passers-by tuning in. Since youngsters are usually keenly interested in any communication between a teacher and one of their peers, they cannot resist the temptation to eavesdrop. It is absurd for a teacher to assume that other pupils are not listening simply because he has told them to go on with their work. How many of us miss the opportunity to pick up some juicy tidbit if we don't have to listen through the wall or peek through the keyhole?

A group works well together when its members come to know, understand, and trust each other. Trust cannot be commanded or legislated, it must grow. Most of us have learned plenty about whom not to trust. Even young children must do some unlearning before they can feel safe and trusting in a classroom. A genuinely democratic learning community is a good place for trust to grow. You may not love everyone in it but you can begin to trust them as you become more worthy of their trust. Violation of trust, by accident or intention, really hurts. If the occurrence is relatively rare, however, the joy experienced in the atmosphere of trust will outweigh the temporary discomfort of having it violated. It is very difficult for the teacher to learn to trust; in our culture it is considered all right for young people to lean on older people but not the reverse. And the trust does at times resemble dependency. In any event, we wish you luck; we too are both still working hard at unlearning old patterns so that we can trust and be trusted freely and openly.

Each of us lives in many communities: our place of work, our neighborhood, our circle of friends, our family, our town or city, as well as the state, the nation, and the world. School can do a lot to get us ready for full and satisfying participation in all of them.

It is easy to fall into the trap of thinking that the sole purpose of school is to prepare youngsters for more advanced studies. Not everyone goes to college and graduate school, and even those who do must live as human beings. The ability to solve problems in ways that bring them joy would be a marvelous accomplishment toward which the school could contribute, for instance, by helping them learn to live with themselves and others; to find satisfaction in work, and renewal in creative leisure time activities; to bring aid and comfort to their fellow men; to explore the outer limits of love; and to settle fights without murder, or war. These are worthy goals, and school can help toward them.

But school merely provides the place; the job is in the hands of a professional called a teacher.

Good luck!

3

Human Solutions for Common Problems in the Classroom Community

Although this is not a "how to" book in the usual sense of that term, we hope that its broad guidelines will help you cope more effectively with some of the many nagging problems that arise from time to time in the classroom. The material has been distilled from our experience, including plenty of mistakes. We all know that there is no easy road to effective teaching. The make-up of each classroom differs greatly from all those before and to come after, but certain problems, like death and taxes, seem inevitable.

Problems are alive, and a person without them is dead, or might as well be. Learning to solve problems is an *essential* part of growing. You, the teacher, are there to help students learn to cope with problems without getting stuck yourself. We have no magic solutions or quick cures. The best we can hope for is that you will think seriously about the problems, gain a better perspective, and handle them by drawing from your own deep well of experience.

We recommend that you use all available good help in arranging for your students' educational needs. If an appropriate specialist is at hand—a school psychologist, psychiatrist, or social worker—by all means enlist his aid in dealing with psychological problems and conflicts in the classroom. In that case, the advice offered here may still help you to refine your own thinking about how to handle various classroom situations.

Many problems can keep children from using their learning capabilities to the fullest. Their lives are closely interwoven with those of their parents, siblings, peers and teachers. Viewing any one problem in isolation as the cause of some barrier to learning is a dangerous oversimplification. Humans are more complex than that. Youngsters need your help in learning to solve their problems because there is no magic formula. Problems are useful to them if they become sufficiently skillful to avoid being engulfed by these difficulties and thereby stunted in emotional growth.

Certain problems arise because of the vast differences between a pupil's ghetto environment and the average teacher's middle-class environment. This point cannot be overemphasized in schools that serve neighborhoods experiencing direct sociological and economic pressures. The teacher will find it hard to be effective if he is revolted by ghetto smells or alienated by the pupils' use of language for which he would have been severely punished as a child.

Adults working with children often begin by asking, "Why in the world does Johnny act that way?" and then proceed to look for reasons in inherited characteristics, environmental factors, or past events. "Is his family economically disadvantaged?" "Did he have too little time to enjoy and be enjoyed by his parents before his siblings took over?" "Is he able to accept his color, his cultural identity, or a physical defect?" "Is he without a father at home?" These questions turn up interesting answers but it is far more productive to find out what Johnny expects to accomplish with his behavior. In other words, what are his goals and how does he believe he is moving toward them?

The youngster's course may seem erratic and without signposts to others, but it must appear reasonable to him. It behooves the teacher to search out these hidden goals. His life style, the composite of all behavior and attitudes, is usually determined by the time he enters school. Since Johnny's chosen course may lead him to abysmal failure, multiplying rather than removing the barriers to learning and maturation, the teacher can best help him by encouraging him to recognize the dysfunctioning in his own life style.

The following rules of thumb, in no particular order, may help you deal with problems we have not discussed separately.

1. *When faced with problem behavior, ask more than "Why?".* What is the youngster trying to say with this problem? What does he gain by his actions? What does this tell me of his needs? How could he satisfy these needs more constructively? Can *I* help him find another way? Or, who else might? He may be putting into behavior what he cannot get into words. To whom is he saying it? Who ultimately gets his message? Is his behavior seemingly aimed at peers, authority figures, parents, or someone else?

2. *If you are not sure what to do, say so, and delay significant action if possible.* Problems are rarely as urgent as they seem. The boy in the back row who has shouted an obscene remark will still be in the same class tomorrow, and you will have had more time to think. You can let him know that you heard him and are not sure what to do about it. Someone else in the class may have some helpful ideas.

3. *There is no such thing as a problem child.* Every youngster has serious problems and therefore causes problems. We have to help him seek solutions. Pinning on him such a label too often adds still another burden because others see him as troublesome.

4. *Problems stimulate learning.* Unless a youngster feels hopelessly blocked, or someone tries to give him ready-made answers, he will seek his own solution and thereby learn something about how to attack future problems. The search for solutions builds strength.

5. *There is no right answer.* Every problem, like its owner, is unique, and the solution must be unique. Two youngsters may exhibit the same problem behavior for quite different reasons. An experienced teacher does not offer cellophane-wrapped answers because he knows they will not help the youngsters to weather future storms.

6. *When troubled by a youngster's behavior, look into your own feelings and behavior in the same area at the same age.* What seems to the teacher to be problem behavior may merely reflect some unresolved problem in his own past. If this is the case he can start solving it without bothering the students.

7. *The class is a community in which you are a leader but not a ruler.* As leader of a group made up of ever-changing subgroups, you can help the community deal with problems and can exert the necessary social pressure to control individual impulses. You are responsible for the creation of class structure, for defining certain limits and certain kinds of appropriate behavior, but it would be inappropriate, even if it were possible, for you to solve community problems by edict.

SOME RECURRING PROBLEMS

ADOPTION

This particular problem area does not arise in school but the effects are evident there, nonetheless. A youngster brings the news that a baby sister was born the night before in the hospital. Another youngster joins in by saying that he was born at home because his mother could not get to the hospital in time. Another child says, perhaps with a questioning note in his voice, "I didn't grow inside my mother and get born; I was adopted." After a moment of uneasy silence, the activities continue. This youngster has posed his question, and clearly exposed to peers and teachers his search for identity, which he feels is a little different from that of his classmates. He is asking for help in his quest and the sensitive teacher will keep this in mind and be better prepared when the matter comes up the next time. A simple statement such as: "Each of us started life growing inside our mother's body. Yes, a lot of people are adopted, but all of us grew inside *someone*."

When a tender spot in someone else's life is exposed, we want to help him, but may retract for fear of offending. We have found that this approach works well in many different situations: First, simply let him know that you have heard him, are aware of the problem and not terrified by it, that you know it can be dealt with like any other serious difficulty, and that he can grow stronger by learning how to deal with it. If you pull back and do not respond to a youngster's half-hidden SOS, he interprets your response to read, "Your problem is so terrible, I don't even want to acknowledge it." This obviously does not help him find the courage to attack it.

Secondly, we favor responding directly to all questions and correcting any erroneous statements that come out. Do not go further and, above all, do not launch into a big lecture. Give what is asked for in words the youngster can clearly understand; overwhelming him with words may obscure the points you want to make. You have probably heard about the child who asked his father, "What is sex?" At the end of a half-hour lecture on birds, bees, and love, he said in bewilderment, "But the line on the page after 'sex' is even smaller than the lines after 'name' and 'address'." The moral is to make sure you understand the question and check along the way to make sure that the youngster understands your answer.

Adoption is an emotionally charged area for the teacher as well as the student. You should ask yourself, "What is the truth here and how can I say it as simply as possible?" If instead you look for words to minimize the child's hurt, you will be caught in a thicket of lies or half-truths that will keep him from meeting the problem forthrightly. The truth is that our society hurts adopted children, by assuming that they were all born out of wedlock, that the parents were too poor to keep them, that the mother died, or that the circumstances were what we secretly think of as shameful. Anything that could cause a mother to give up her child is suspect; even death is something we are embarrassed about.

Imagine a primitive society in which a youngster's natural biological mother did not want or could not keep him, so he was given to another mother who wanted him. He sees both mothers every day, although his biological mother pays little attention to him. Everyone in the village ignores the situation because they have pressing concerns such as finding enough food for the community. The child may be hurt by his real mother's indifference but he can see that it is her nature, and meanwhile he has another mother who cares deeply for him. He has a hurtful problem, principally the sad truth about his natural mother, which he has to learn to accept and cope with as he matures.

In our "advanced" society, however, things are not so easy. We have adoption agencies. The transfer of human life is handled with efficient dignity. The new parents do not know the biological parents and vice versa. An adopted youngster never knows his roots. He may question strange women often in an obsessive way: "What is your name? Do you have little children? Where do you live? Are all your children living with you?" Searching for his roots, he is asking, "Are you my real mother?" We must be truthful with him, usually a sad task. He must learn that adoption agencies believe it is better for adopted children not to know about or see their biological parents.

Until recently, the adoptive process was overemphasized and overglamorized. Before the child even knew the word adoption, the parents said: "We saw you, liked you, you were the most beautiful child, so we adopted you." Some families even celebrated two occasions, the child's actual birth date and the adoption date. Now we are beginning to dole out information in smaller doses, as the child seeks it and with less sugar-coating.

All that talk about choosing the very best baby can easily turn a child's thoughts to times when these parents have let him know quite clearly that he is acting like a monster and they do not like him. If they brought him home through an act of will, they could always change their minds, and take him back through another act of will. Furthermore, his biological parents, whom he probably never knew, gave him up before he was adopted. It is a genuine problem; heavy sugar-coating makes any healthy youngster imagine that it is too complex and dreadful for him to understand.

School is a place, or should be, for sorting out what is true from confused misunderstandings, if learning is to have any meaning at all. "Why didn't my real mother keep me?" The truth from the teacher is something like, "I don't know. I don't know anything about your real mother. I know something about *you* though. I bet if we put our heads together we could think of some reasons why mothers sometimes have to give up their children."

Other situations pop up. "Johnny says I'm adopted because I never had any father." "Johnny's full of baloney," says the teacher, "Everyone in this world had a father as well as a mother, even if we don't all still have them both. If you didn't have a father and a mother you couldn't have been born."

A youngster's quest for his natural parents must be accepted, though our society has blocked his path. Once accepted, the less said about it and the adoption process the better. Everyone in the class can learn something from a discussion about the parents who really take care of them day in and day out, whether they are biological parents, adoptive parents, or foster parents. The more emphasis is placed on the parents who feed, raise and educate him, the more his adoption can be taken in stride.

Perhaps we ought to add that it is destructive to even *hint* that he should be grateful to his adoptive or foster parents. He had no control over his conception or birth (as youngsters often point out to parents who seem to expect repayment for the gift of life); he usually had no control over adoption or placement in a foster home; so why should he feel grateful? Our society wrongs out-of-wedlock children from the time of conception, then tries to make amends by assuming the responsibility for their care after birth. If he were not in his home, he would be in another home or in an institution.

Adopted and foster children are more sensitive than their peers to disposition of a dog or other "adopted" family pet. If the pet is given away the child believes that the same thing could happen to him.

A number of children in ghetto areas, white and black alike, never knew their fathers because of desertion or illegitimacy and are often amazed to learn that without a father they would not be in this world.

BODY ODOR, CLEANLINESS, AND OBESITY

Numerous problems related to the care and feeding of our bodies crop up in the classroom. A common complaint of the teacher in a ghetto school is, "I could do more teaching if I could bear to get nearer to the children; they smell so bad that I keep my distance." Teachers have the same complaint about one or two students in a classroom in a middle-class or well-to-do school area. What can be done about the child who smells bad? We could turn the question around, of course, and ask what the student can do about the teacher who smells bad. That is not as silly as it seems at first blush. The odors given off by human bodies are pleasant or unpleasant, depending upon the "smeller." A highly scrubbed, de-odorized, and perfumed teacher can be very objectionable to a youngster accustomed to natural human odors. We think it can be largely the teacher's problem and may have to be made a part of a health unit on personal grooming.

What it boils down to is that our reactions to human odors vary so widely that some sort of compromise must be reached. Compromise is seldom successful, however, if one of the parties involved believes he is completely right and the other is completely wrong. One misconception to be clarified before discussions get started is that no human body can be odorless. Every body has odors which come in a wide variety. Many television viewers, after years of commercials, have learned to scrub away natural odors or to mask them with manufactured scents. You may change one set for another, but your body still has odors.

You can start a discussion in class about whether each youngster, if blindfolded, could identify his classmates by odors alone. It will help to bring home the point that everyone has odors and that they differ widely. You might even participate in the game yourself. The language in such a discussion has to be tailored to fit the age level. Let us keep in mind the large families with one bathroom, with chronic bed-wetters (no matter what the reason), or children who sleep in their underwear and continue to wear it day after day.

Once this basic lesson in relativity is grasped, a youngster's smell may still be offensive to you, even though you can better accept him in this respect. If the general discussion is unproductive, you might have a heart-to-heart talk in which you say that his odors and yours may not match very well; you're having a hard time getting used to his and suspect that he may have the same difficulty with yours. You've been wondering if you could do anything to make yourself more pleasant to him by using cosmetics with another scent, or perhaps with less scent than your present ones. It would be helpful, you continue, if he could use some kind of commercial deodorant or scrub away his natural odors more often because you are having a hard time getting used to them. The more genuine your respect for him, as reflected in your words, the more chance there is of success in this kind of talk. Remember, you are asking a favor— that he accommodate to *your* needs, not because you are more right or good but because you are entitled to your individual needs and to ask for help in meeting them. If you simply communicate "you smell bad," he quite naturally feels hurt and considers you presumptuous in the bargain.

Cleanliness is another habit that is relative. Many, many people in our world bathe once a week at most, and there is little evidence of damage to their health from this factor alone. The difference between your own and your students' body cleaning habits may bring you into conflict. If so, the conflict should be handled with maximum respect for dignity and rights on both sides. They are neither wrong nor bad if their washing habits differ from yours, and they may have different problems.

Body odors and cleaning habits are closely related and may cause particular difficulties in a ghetto. Even when a student accepts the need for frequent cleaning of his body and clothing, the household plumbing facilities in relation to the size of the family may make this extremely difficult if not impossible. Sometimes the bathroom is shared with several other large families. No washing machine may be available, the sink and clothes-hanging facilities may be limited and the laundromat too expensive. A youngster can do his best to cope with these realistic problems yet not be entirely successful. It would be well for you to be genuinely understanding; it may be far easier for you to adjust to his odors than for him to accommodate to your needs.

You, the teacher, might well ponder the relative impact of menstrual odors (or powders to mask them), or garlic and onion, or Juicy Fruit chewing gum, or overpowering perfume, or halitosis.

It may prove impossible to discuss what you consider personal problems in this line with each student in the class, but the whole subject could be brought into the frame of reference of a health education unit conducted by the school nurse.

Obesity is another signal that a youngster is unaware of or unable to meet other people's expectations of him. People get fat for various reasons, of which one of the most common is that food becomes a substitute for other gratifications. A child in a classroom providing a great deal of affection and emotional support may be less likely to stuff himself with food. Obesity is due to many other factors as well. Almost all middle-class women (and most of the men) in the United States are overweight because delicious food is easily obtained and they have less physical activity each year as more and more machines take over human work.

Sometimes a chubby person is not at all aware of the impression he makes on others; general discussion about bodies and how we look to others is helpful. We send messages to others by the way we dress, stand, talk, walk, and also by how much we are over (or under) weight. We reveal what we think of ourselves every time we show our bodies in public. But even here the standards are relative. You may be repulsed by very fat or skinny youngsters while they feel just fine about their own bodies. If it is a problem for you, first admit it to yourself. A general discussion may be valuable and, if not, you may want to arrange a personal conference with the child involved and confess your bothersome need. You may not be in a position to ask him to gain or lose weight, any more than you can ask him to wash more often or smell differently, but you can share with him your difficulty in being physically close to him. The information may interest him, and he may even care enough about you to try to do something about the problem that disturbs you.

The two key words in the area of care and feeding of one's body are relativity and dignity. Offense is in the eye or the nose of the beholder. In trying to cope with it, it is bad taste to threaten the dignity of the other person.

CHEATING

In any classroom, cheating is a common but deceptively complex problem for a teacher. To start with, it's a good idea to look behind the immediate incident for clues. Why did Maud, or Jim, or Tony cheat on a test yesterday? Why would anyone want to cheat?

Clues in individual cases may be hard to track down but the general causes of cheating are easier to find. In a school setting, the best grades usually go to a student whose answers, not whose questions, we approve of. He is seldom commended for saying "I don't know" or for an ingenious, resourceful answer.

In a "go-get-it" society, the youngsters obtaining the best grades is on the track leading to prestige and money. He will eat better, live in a better home, and be treated with much more respect than a peer who merely tries to satisfy his curiosity.

A student who sorts out his confusion on an exam paper rarely sees a comment like, "Good try! At least you're much clearer now about what you don't know." Instead he is likely to find a red F, followed by "Incorrect" or "You did not answer the question asked." This being the case, what can you expect of a student? What did you do throughout your school years? You probably worked for "right" answers and good grades and very likely cheated at least once along the way.

We teachers are stuck unless we can look our students squarely in the eye and say that the fun of learning rests on finding new areas of ignorance. We must be able to convey our genuine excitement about discovering a new area about which we knew little or nothing. As long as we treat questions as embarrassing and shameful evidence that someone does not already know the answers, we are stuck. Insane as it may be, recognition and approval depend on knowing all the answers; the youngster who can create that image even by cheating should therefore have the greatest reward. If he is caught, of course, his whole house of cards falls. But in our culture, there is a big temptation to take the chance and cheat in the hope of getting away with it. What a mess for a teacher! Cheating will continue in the classroom as long as "right" answers head the list of academic values.

The teacher is put in a bind here. If class scores are composed at the end of the year, he is likely to have them in mind and stress this kind of learning to please the principal. If the teacher can be persuaded that students will perform well even though given varied kinds of tests during the year, he might courageously try. However, teachers do not have much faith in children because they don't encounter many people who have faith in them in the school situation, be they parents, colleagues, or principal.

Within this general framework, the reasons for cheating vary. Pete, the one in the back row with the striped shirt, cheats for obvious reasons. His glasses slide down his nose three times every five minutes; while pushing them back in place, he leans awkwardly toward the bright girl in the purple sweater. When you meet his parents you begin to understand. They are determined on Harvard, Yale, or Princeton; he knows he will disappoint them because he cannot even manage long division. Like many worried children, he is a realist. Disaster is inevitable, but if he applies himself by cheating on exams and faking between times, he may be a couple of years further along the road before his parents discover that their son is not too bright. The price he pays for borrowed time is that everyone meanwhile finds out he also lies and cheats. This is a contemporary tragedy. He believes he invented cheating in the evil core of his being; he is too unsophisticated to realize how subtly everyone in his world has taught him to play this shameful game.

Can you help him? Not if you believe that correct answers to questions on the exam indicate a student's worth. Or as long as your worth as a teacher is gauged by the student's correct answers.

However, if you honestly believe that each person's special individual worth bears no relation to how well he answers questions, you can help Pete to come to terms with his problem in the course of a school year. With less pressure from home and school he can afford to take inventory of his assets. Conferences with his parents can help enormously. The purpose is not to convey "I'm terribly sorry to say that Pete isn't bright enough for an Ivy League college," but rather, "Pete is suffering because we are not giving him a chance to be himself, recognize his talents, and find out where he wants to go in life." You might point out what you know already about his assets: He helped to organize the last class outing and his ability to assemble details into meaningful patterns plus his limitless patience could lead to a prestigious position in various fields. There is a good chance that the parents will join in helping Pete to appreciate his positive qualities without helping him to perform in areas where he does not feel competent. Push anyone too hard to be an all-round winner and he may well turn out to be an all-round mess.

Or how about the thirteen-year-old girl with the crib notes hidden everywhere imaginable? She does not know Ivy League from poison ivy but knows what it means to be "left back" and she has had a whirl in the so-called *opportunity* class. She has been laughed at enough in her life, and is taking no chances. Even if she is caught cheating, her peers won't laugh. They may think she is not very nice, but they will have to admire her cunning. Why take a chance on remembering something when she can be sure of reading it from her palmed notes?

As her teacher, you can assure this student that your classroom is a place where people do not laugh at or think less of a person who doesn't know something. You can also urge her to trust her mind and memory. It will take a lot of time and patience and many gentle rewards for the timidly asked questions and the mumbled hunches. Comments such as "Better luck next time" may only make her clam up because she knows her "next times" are limited. Your task is to repair damage done in previous years of schooling.

There is the quiet high-school junior with the harelip. Her eyes follow you every minute; she adores you. Cheating appalls her but she feels an even greater risk would be your disapproval if you were to see through to her "real" self. She wants to follow in your footsteps, and you seem to know all the answers. An admission of honest ignorance on your part now and then could do a lot to disabuse her of this idea. A personal gesture, *e.g.*, an occasional magazine clipping brought from home on a subject that interests her, might not be amiss. You are letting her see that you too are seeking answers, also that you know she is there and you care about her. A sociogram might reveal material leading to possible bridges to her peers.

Cheating can crop up in a clique of bright, affluent students who compete in it as a creative sport. Wherever the problem appears, handling it involves honest regard for the individual's worth, not for how many questions he can answer. Your aim is to convince students that *not knowing* is a greater challenge than *knowing*. Cheating is a sympton of intellectual disease. Rewards must exist for searching and questioning. If a student cannot hold his head high during his precious years on our planet, we teachers have failed him. He cheats to present himself in a light different from the true one. Must any of your students live with such lack of dignity?

CLOTHING AND HAIR STYLES

Have your own hair and clothing styles changed in the past ten or fifteen years? If so, you have been conforming to national trends.

If not, you may be using these styles as a means of self-expression or a display of individualism. Elementary school students tend to follow the dictates of their parents in regard to matters of hair or clothing, but junior high and high school students are tuned in to peer norms.

Just as the style-conscious teacher reads *Bazaar* or *Gentlemen's Quarterly* to see what is "in," pre-teens and teenagers laboriously study their peers in the classroom, on the street, and in television and movies. They tend to follow guidelines set by their particular style kings and queens. They are conformists, though they seem to be non-conformists because they shun the guidelines of adults. A few refuse to be led by their peers or by adults, setting their own styles and asserting their own individuality.

During the past decade, the junior style setters (teens and pre-teens) have permitted widely contrasting tastes to operate. Within certain broad limits, it is considered chic (hip, cool, groovy) to dress differently from everyone else. This seems to be a healthy step toward genuine release of excessive pressure to conform.

Clothing and hair styles call attention to the individual, add to his natural physical assets, or offer a place for him to hide. It would be hard to build any other case for clothing in this day of over-heating, air conditioning, and mass transit, which would permit people to go nude except for donning a warm wrap to go from building to transportation on a particularly chilly day. We do not go nude, however; we want to hide or enhance our natural body. As part of their general education, youngsters can be urged to think about how and why they wish to decorate their bodies.

The teacher who demands that a youngster change his clothing or hair style because it is in "inherently bad taste" is in an embarrassing spot for a supposed model of an educated person. The history teacher caught in this spot is bizarre. History or contemporary anthropology reveals that such styles vary widely at different times and places on our planet; at any given moment and in any given place, the uneducated and ignorant citizens have considered the current style a mark of inherent good taste while the person with broader horizons considered it simply a mark of conformity.

It is perfectly reasonable for an educator to want students to think about why they choose certain clothing or hair styles. Such discussion can lead them to examine other values in life and to come

closer to understanding their own self-concept. For an educator to
say, "Your hair is too long," or "Your skirt is too short," implies
that there is some celestial standard for determining the right length
for each. If he is worried that too-short skirts will provoke boys to
uncontrollable expressions of lust, he ought to say so. The girls may
continue to wear short skirts either because they disagree or would
like to experience the boys' lust. The educator may feel that he is
legally and morally responsible for the girl's physical well-being;
if he demands that they avoid provoking the boy's lustful expressions, whether they want to or not, he will have to cite reasons for
his belief that they are in physical danger. He wants his students to
see that he, as an educated person, is influenced more by evidence
than by hunches when it comes to decisions affecting their behavior.

He may believe that long hair on boys is a physical hazard if
they are working near machinery or driving in convertibles. If he
warns them of the danger and they ignore the warning, he may consider it his moral and legal responsibility to demand that they cut
or cover their hair for safety's sake. Again, he should cite the evidence so that they can observe the model of the educated man in
action.

The truth of the matter is that an educator, being human, has
his soft spots and blind spots. If he grew up in an age when young
men wore short hair, it seems somehow wrong or unmanly for his
students to suddenly sprout shoulder-length hair. Similar reactions
from his colleagues and other contemporaries reinforce his belief
that this type of grooming is bad. He is likely to issue warnings and
then perhaps get into a power struggle with them which would
make him look pretty silly in future history books. Keep in mind
that if George and Martha Washington were to be reincarnated and
come to dinner, they might find your lack of good taste in hair and
dress styles quite unsettling.

This area of conflict between generations provides a marvelous
opportunity for youngsters and their elders to listen to each other's
reasoning and become more articulate in communication. Every
youngster *must* be different from members of the previous generation. How else can he begin to taste independence? It is a relatively
immature way of proving to oneself that he has grown up. He fol-
lows a different drummer, watches his elders squirm, and is reassured to find they can do nothing about it. This separation process
is especially hard on members of the older generation if the lines of

communication are not kept open. Since language is another item subject to style changes, the educator anxious to open communication will find it helpful to keep saying, "Do you mean such and such . . . ?" until he feels sure he understands what the younger person is conveying.

Any attempt by older persons to seize control of a youngster's expressive means of decorating his body is resented, but he should know how his "decorations" affect them, *e.g.*, that a particular costume may make both his father and mother embarrassed to be seen publicly with him. He can then make a choice, and so can they. If he chooses not to change the costume, they have the choice of going or not going out with him. If their choice not to go bothers him, he may have to rethink his decision to keep his costume; if it does not bother him, they must go separate ways in public. If this separateness upsets the parents, sharing the feeling with him may make some difference. And so it goes. Each of us should strive for control over self and not over others, unless they are doing something that threatens their own or another's physical well-being. But sharing our feelings with people we care for *may* influence their behavior.

DEATH

A class is almost always touched by death during the school year. One youngster's mother may die of cancer, another's father may die of a heart attack, or a grandmother may succumb to the ailments of old age. The death may be in the teacher's own family or in the group of classroom pets. Death is a part of human experience and cannot be ignored.

Human reaction to death often includes a mixture of fear, anger, sadness, and denial. Even if we, as teachers, foolishly try to ignore death, these feelings will be there. They are less easily pushed aside than the feelings accompanying other human experiences because death, in our culture, is a potent taboo. We are all drawn to it, as to any dark secret. It provides a good opportunity to expand learning in the classroom because it catches everyone's interest in a compelling way. How the learning is handled varies with the student's age level and past experiences, but some general guidelines may be worth remembering.

Very young children do not understand death and its associated cultural rituals in the same way as an adult. They know life vividly through their senses. If they have seen or heard about a cemetery, they may strongly suspect that people are living there under the ground. Through class discussion, children can be helped to understand that after death, one's body can no longer taste, feel, see, hear, or experience any sensation. They need, and are entitled to, adult reassurance that children very rarely die; that people usually die when old (from the child's vantage point). If pressed, you must admit that children do sometimes die but it is most unusual. It is important for the child not to "walk scared" even in a potentially dangerous world. On the other hand, we must not lie to him about this fundamental subject (or, if possible, about any other subjects).

Rural children have more opportunity than their urban counterparts to see and cope with death in a natural setting. Animals die or are killed by other animals. Unfortunately, city children may observe their fellow human beings as "killing" animals, and older students, rural and urban, have ample evidence that men kill each other over ideas—a terribly important point to be examined in school.

Because he sees death often and may even perform crude autopsies, even a young country child usually grasps the totality of death. He has reason to believe that the senses no longer function after death. This is one of the important functions of animal pets in the classroom. If one of them dies it is a good idea not to remove the body immediately but to give the children time to understand that it is a truly dead body. Let the children handle the dead animal freely during the day; if it was a beloved pet, their sadness is natural and should be recognized. If the animal was being kept by older children as part of a science experiment, the science teacher might perform an autopsy which the children can watch or not, depending on their wishes. We are, after all, working in the area of a cultural taboo. A child who is not ready for an autopsy this year may be ready next year.

After ignorance, fear is the thing to watch for. When death is in the air, each of us asks if we may not be next. (Again, even very young children cannot be reasonably sure that this is unlikely.) This kind of fear helps to prepare a growing youngster for his job: to protect himself, to anticipate the future, to learn and grow through anticipation. Our job as teachers is to help him express and acknowledge his fear, then find truthful reassurance. Fear that stays hidden is much harder to cope with.

Anger is the next big factor connected with death that the teacher is likely to sense. If a person or an animal loved by a child dies, there will be a residue of anger. We adults tend to deny it as irrational and "not nice." How can you be mad at someone or something for dying? A youngster more honestly acknowledges this feeling and expresses it. His thoughts run something like this: "I loved him and he didn't love me, or he wouldn't have left me. He left me even though he knew I'd be hurt. That was very mean. I hate him." This irrational line of reasoning rings a responsive bell in most adults. We may know that the other person could not help dying and leaving us and that our hurt is unreasonable, but there it is; and we have no one to blame. A peculiar kind of anger is involved, but we usually do not label it as such because it would seem too ridiculous.

The anger, like the fear, can help a youngster grow if it is expressed and acknowledged. This does not mean that it is sufficient for a teacher to point out to a youngster that he has such feelings. It may be a big help for the entire class or the youngster himself to acknowledge that we all have angry and fearful feelings at times. When they arise in the classroom, we might ask the students to draw a picture, write a story, or describe a happening in their lives with the theme of anger, fear or frustration. In class discussion afterward, they can share their various feelings and experiences. In case it seems very clear that a youngster is talking about fear or anger and hasn't found the proper words, you might chance saying, "It sounds as if you mean you're scared or mad, or both." If he is ready to wear the shoe it will fit; if not, you can forget it.

Above all, a teacher would do well not to react with horror or even surprise when a youngster taps and expresses his fear or anger about death. Most of us have been inculcated with the idea that speaking ill of the dead is wrong and will increase our guilt. If one can verbalize the anger while it is fresh, and if it is accepted and easily understood by valued persons in his life, the anger may be drained off without his suffering later guilt. It is then over and done with, instead of seeping out like a secret poison in the days and years ahead.

Another human reaction associated with death is denial. Because death is such a basic human phenomenon and affects each of us so deeply, a great deal of pretending is connected with it. We pretend in order to avoid the strong feelings we fear will control us, rather than the other way around. We pretend to feel happy that old uncle has gone to his rich reward. We truly loved him and so we turn to a child who also loved him and smilingly explain the wonderful thing that happened to uncle.

The child sees red-rimmed swollen eyes with dark circles, and other physiological signs of grief; he is not fooled. Your body tells him you feel anything but joyful regardless of your words and forced smile. What conclusion can he possibly draw? If you, a trustworthy adult, must lie to him about your feelings, death must be truly dreadful. Chances are that he will not speak to you honestly and openly about death again. He and his peers will try to figure out the magic and ritual attending something so important that it must be masked with secrecy. And conversely, if a learning youngster is confronted with an adult who is relieved at being finally rid of a relationship that was hateful or, at best, a mixed bag, but is pretending sorrow and grief, what conclusions can he draw?

The feelings of sadness over a death that touches a classroom are easier to deal with because they are acceptable. But we may need to give the youngsters more opportunity for expression and recognition than is usually the case. The important thing is to help them air their true feelings and ask their questions when confronted with death. Teachers do well to strip away pretense and secrecy whenever possible, particularly with a subject as profoundly important as death.

DISRESPECT

Teachers and other adults around the world are troubled by disrespectful or "sassy" children. The best place to start coming to terms with this problem is with yourself. Adults with a large fund of self-respect need few tokens of respect from the outside world, while those with a small fund usually search feverishly for evidences of respect. It is as if being called by a particular title or shown deference in other ways makes him feel superior and therefore deserving of respect. This upside-down kind of emotional reasoning is never sufficiently reassuring. The person continues to be supersensitive to any presumed or real slights from those he meets daily.

Almost all of us have learned the hard way that respect is earned and cannot be demanded. Your intrinsic worth places you naked before the world no matter what your titles, possessions, or bank balance. You can, like the rest of mankind, try to improve yourself and thus raise your self-esteem. As you value yourself more, others will usually follow suit. "Doing your thing" may offend some people, but your integrity will win their respect even if it is grudging and silent.

In other words, if you believe a youngster is being disrespectful, you might ask yourself just what you would like from him. If some soul searching reveals that you depend upon him for the respect you cannot give yourself, it is a good idea to get off his back. If you seek signs of respect for your own sake (whatever the reasons) rather than for his, you'd probably better stop where you are. As teachers, we are interested in meeting the student's needs before our own.

We do not suggest that genuine disrespect go unnoticed. If a youngster sticks out his tongue at you and says, "Shove it, Teach!" something should be done. One of the first things, of course, is to try to find out why he is being so rude. And by the way, the answer to "Why are you being so rude, Alfie?" is likely to be loud laughter —mainly because some other kind of response is expected from you. A child exhibiting rude, provocative behavior usually expects to have the involved person strike back. The laughter may make you feel silly and less able to deal reasonably with the situation; a neutral response that deals with it honestly can lead to the answers you seek.

You might say in a neutral unthreatening tone, "I don't like it when people talk to me that way" or "Tell me what you dislike and maybe I can do something about it." You are not striking back but merely registering your rights as one citizen in the classroom community. You might go further by saying, "It lets me know you're angry at me but gives me no chance to find out why or try to iron things out."

A more expected response such as "One more rude word out of your foul mouth and you're going straight to the office," starts the kind of interesting war the young man probably wants, but it is not conducive to growth for him, his classmates, or the teacher.

Being truly helpful to a disrespectful child calls for some detective work. What kind of response was he expecting? If he was seeking it, did something going on between parent and child suddenly spill over into the classroom? Or did his performance have something to do with his peers who were watching avidly?

A classroom, like any other community, must adopt some rules for mutual respect. The teacher cannot simply announce them; all the citizens must agree, and they will not buy the package unless there is something in it for them. A teacher who demands that children stand and say "good morning" cheerfully to any adult entering the room is rarely willing to go through this ritual when any child enters the room. Children sense the second-class citizenship implied and may go along with it because of possible punishment for breaking the rules, but they can hardly be expected to learn anything that will contribute toward their self-respect. If teachers or other adults are entitled to special forms of respect that are not offered in return to students, the reasons must be clearly spelled out. Local code aside, we cannot think of any good reasons.

We believe a teacher has the right to be respected as an individual. You may be interested in helping a youngster in your class but his spitting, cursing, or sneering constitutes a bar. We have had some success with an honest approach, geared to the age of the child, such as, "Look, Claude, I know you're acting that way for some reason. I'd like to help you but your behavior really gets under my skin. If you'll try to control it, I'll try to be of help. If you can't or won't, maybe someone else in the class has suggestions. But if it continues, I can't stay in the same room with you. One of us will have to go, and that probably means you'll have to be transfered to another class."

Where things go from there depends a great deal upon the youngster and his classmates. He knows you have honestly told him where you stand. That is useful for his learning and may be the best you can do for him at that particular time.

Disrespect, like a fight, involves two people; hopefully, the teacher can rally professional resources in the situation rather than simply striking back like another child.

DIVORCE AND SEPARATION

Jerome, a black boy in kindergarten who usually has a smile that lights the world, becomes more quiet day by day for almost an entire week. While he is drawing one day, he looks up at you and says, "My Daddy and Mama are buying a divorce."

The plain blond girl in your fourth grade to whom no one pays much attention begins to fidget and squirm. She forgets her homework and does not hear your questions. You ask her to stay after school and tell her you are worried about her. She bursts into tears and says that her mother and father have separated. She is living with her father and her mother has gone to another city.

And that lumbering, none-too-bright but terribly good-natured and good-looking athlete in your high school English class begins to get into trouble with everyone. According to the coach, he no longer shows up for football practice and has been in several minor fights in the halls. A girl he has dated confides that his parents are getting a divorce.

This is no longer an unusual situation. Bruno Bettelheim, among others, claims that people stay married about as many years as they did in the nineteenth century; divorce and separation are much more frequent because "until death do us part" does not end the marriage contract as quickly as it used to. Adults in our culture seem to search for new patterns permitting more than one deeply intimate relationship during their life span, which is steadily lengthening with better nutrition and medical care. Whatever the moralistic issues involved, this cultural transition is hard on the children.

Our advice here may be applicable to numerous other situations in which youngsters experience an emotional ache they can do little about; they have no say in their parent's decision to stay together or separate; just as in other situations, they can do nothing about the reality factor responsible for their distress.

Very young children need to express their fear of being abandoned; their sorrow, anger and guilt. Since they cannot put their feelings into words, children may express them through painting, drawing, clay modeling, creative play, or simply through a flood of tears following some minor incident. We believe the best policy is simply to let the feelings come out without probing or interpreting. Your main value may be to provide experiences that foster expression of feeling, instead of the "listen, watch, and learn" kind that demand attention and block expression of feeling.

As children grow older and more accustomed to words, they may need a good listener—one who does not evaluate, judge, or preach, but lets the talker know that his feelings are being perceived as well as his words.

Still more mature youths need the opportunity to sort out their feelings and thoughts in genuinely free discussion. This is not to be confused with a teacher-led pseudo-discussion that is really a laborious attempt to state a moral such as, "When people don't take responsibility in love, they hurt themselves and others," or a foolish attempt to heal with empty wisdom, such as, "It's always darkest before the dawn."

Upset youngsters need to drain off pent-up feelings that accumulate in a situation beyond their control. They wonder if any of their peers can understand what is happening inside them, and what it will mean in their future lives. Free discussion provides the necessary opportunities; little can be accomplished by talking *at* them or telling them how to go about feeling better.

We have tried to point out that as the youngster matures, he tends to move from nonverbal expression, to confiding, to discussion, but there are no clear division lines; all three are present in some degree in his time of need. The kindergartner's needs may be expressed largely nonverbally, but he may also confide in you and even try discussion. The reverse would probably be true of high school students who might enjoy a discussion in an appropriate setting but also need to confide and perhaps react nonverbally by painting a picture or punching someone in the nose.

We have found it effective to be rather offhand about making opportunities for expression, confiding, or discussion; to be as sensitive as possible to the youngster's veiled requests without forcing opportunities down his throat. If you push him, he will simply have the added problem of dealing with a nosy teacher. The discussion will come to life only when he feels he can trust the other members of his classroom community; and the confiding will come only when he can trust you. The nonverbal expression will be heavily disguised unless the youngster feels that he can trust himself in school because others trust him. No one would be foolish enough to be trusting simply because a teacher or even a peer said it would be quite safe. Trust is something we start to sniff out while still in the cradle. If it's there, the youngster will feel it; if not, it can't be simulated.

The development of an atmosphere of trust is helped along enormously if the teacher's behavior communicates that he is trying to be worthy of trust. Since he must be able to trust the students, he may risk making himself vulnerable now and then by mentioning some anxieties or hurts that he has overcome to some extent.

Here our advice cannot be specific, because the momentary opportunities for developing trust vary widely and depend upon the particular classroom group. Imagine, however, a teacher whose own parents were divorced, who could admit in a discussion his deep hurt at the time, many times afterward and even now, though it has lessened with the intervening years and his changed perspective as an adult. His admission that the divorce still hurts makes him vulnerable and human, not an all-wise adult who says that time heals all wounds and has healed his completely. He is conveying the idea that such hurts are part of the human experience, and he has felt them keenly. What an opportunity to increase the trust level of the class members! If the teacher can trust them enough to share honest feelings, perhaps they can do the same with him.

You may be uncomfortable about such self-exposure or may consider it unprofessional. Your discomfort reveals something about the atmosphere of trust in your class: you cannot yet trust the other citizens, so it will be that much harder for them to trust you and each other. You may believe that exposing yourself when the trust level of the class is poor would result in pointless hurt. If so, you may need to work on building trust in other ways.

As to the behavior being unprofessional, we believe that being professional means using yourself and any other available "tools" to do the job at hand. The teacher's main task is to facilitate learning. We all know many who hide behind professionalism, pretending to be omniscient and omnipotent gods. This self-protecting device saves them many hurts, but is hardly an asset in carrying out professional tasks. We two also from time to time hide behind professionalism but are conscious of it and trying hard to use this crutch less and less with each passing year. We hope you will do the same.

DRUGS, ALCOHOL, AND TOBACCO

Although they can be physically or emotionally injurious, drugs, alcohol and tobacco are definitely part of the twentieth-century American scene. A growing youngster has to face these problems, and must be helped to find where he stands in relation to each of them.

Most of us over age thirty are very frightened by the drug scene, perhaps because it is the newest threat to our young. We are, with good reason, frightened about the possible ill effects of tobacco, but this habit has been widespread for many years and the tobacco industry's advertising lulls us into a false sense of security. Although we or someone we love may develop lung cancer, a heart condition, or bronchial or circulatory difficulties because of smoking tobacco, we prefer to think the statistics, like those for accidents, refer only to other people—foolish reasoning at best.

The problems of drug usage and addiction penetrate every American school and community, affecting adults as well as youngsters. The many attempts to deal with them have been relatively ineffective. Expelling children from school exposes them to increased seduction by the pushers on the street. School personnel have inflicted severe punishment (including informing the police), lectured *ad nauseum*, and posted catchy slogans to the bulletin boards but have not been able to control, much less conquer, drug problems. School authorities and parents accuse one another of being too lenient or too punitive. We obviously must continue to look for new and different answers or new ways of viewing the problem.

"My experience with young people using drugs," says Asya, "is that if they first use a *large* amount of marijuana or hashish, the ensuing body and mind disturbance is so frightening that they avoid a repetition, at least for some time. In the same way a youngster deeply inhaling his first cigarette usually coughs, chokes, becomes dizzy and wants no part of it. A young person's experimentation with addictive drugs is usually a form of rebellion against authority (in the form of parent, teacher, or the establishment), to prove that he is free and doesn't have to conform to the rules laid down by society. Perhaps we could follow this lead by helping young people find ways of expressing their independence and freedom without endangering their physical or emotional well-being."

"My experience with young people (including teachers)," says Don, "is that marijuana, like alcohol during prohibition, has become the 'in' thing. Very few of them experiment beyond one or two acid (LSD or mescaline) trips or mild forms of speed now and then. The threat here lies in impure, untested drugs. Since use is illegal, there is no way of experimenting safely. Question and answer columns in the underground press provide qualified medical answers to drug questions, but the sad fact is that most of them are un-answerable."

Marijuana usage is widespread and accounts for the greatest amount of upset among parents and teachers. The evidence to date suggests that illegality may be its greatest hazard. There is a good chance that the seller will try to introduce his customers to more expensive and addictive wares such as heroin; he knows they will be steady customers and his profits will be much higher. Then, too, getting into trouble with the police is an ever-present possibility; the future complications could be serious in a society that likes an unblemished public record no matter what goes on behind the scenes.

Our advice to teacher (and parent) is to make sure that a young person is at least aware of these dangers. He should know that his job future may be jeopardized by a record of arrest and/or convic-tion for possession of marijuana. He should know that marijuana sellers may also push addictive drugs and would rather see him hooked on one of them, so he should be wary of their samples and other lures. We know virtually nothing of the long-term cumulative effects of marijuana on the body; it may turn out to be less harmful than alcohol. There is danger in both because of possible impaired judgment, though many people would rather put their lives in the hands of someone stoned on marijuana than someone dead drunk on alcohol.

Ours is a drug-oriented society. We swallow various pills and potions from morning to night. We are bombarded by drug adver-tising in newspapers, magazines, on television, in subways, in buses, and on billboards along the highway. We take things to stay awake, to go to sleep, to curb the appetite, to ease pain, to settle the nerves, to stay healthy, or even to become more sexually attractive. Just think of the number of containers in your medicine cabinet right now. The drug industry makes huge profits and maintains powerful legislative lobbies. Like the comic book publishers who feature sado-masochistic violence as a diet for our young, or the manufacturers of toys and games of war, the industry is not genuinely interested in the damage being done to our civilization. They toss some money out for research or image-boosting advertising but it is a calculated ex-pense designed to keep a concerned public at arm's length.

As long as we live in such a society we must continue to deal patiently with problems of war, sado-masochistic violence, or drug abuse when they affect our youngsters. The best we can do is admit that we can't come to terms with these evils, try to strengthen the youngsters' resolve by giving them heavy doses of truth as we see it at the time, and help them find their own individual ways of coping with these problems.

Truth includes a number of admissions: that most of the advertising flooding our cities is full of lies to get us to spend our money in ways that will make someone else rich; that drugs are unnatural and should be viewed cautiously even when suggested by a prescription-happy, too-busy physician; that we do not yet have evidence that marijuana is physically harmful, though illegality presents other real dangers; that people differ widely in ability to handle alcohol and the same holds true for various drugs; that someone you know has very nearly ruined his life by inability to control his alcohol or drug intake; that while tobacco is legal, many scientists are convinced that it can take years off your life one way or another and result in a painful exit.

But young people are never satisfied with hearing the truth, which is a rare experience, anyway. They wisely distrust someone else's truth; wanting to see, hear, and feel their way toward their own truth. The more adventurous ones are bound to do some experimenting, despite warnings of the dangers, and thereby hurt themselves. In a sense they are foolhardy but we must admire mountain climbers or space explorers. They do not need to take the risks but are willing to do so because they crave first-hand experience.

A safer way is for a youngster to get *almost* first-hand experience by talking to people who have been personally involved with drugs, tobacco smoking, or alcohol. No teetotaller can persuade a heavy drinker to stop; that is why Alcoholics Anonymous is the most successful group in dealing with victims of uncontrolled alcohol consumption. The same is true for drug addiction. No teachers, principal, or other school authority can persuade a beginning addict to give up the habit while he can still do so.

Our hope is that ex-addicts will be employed by schools as resource people. High-school students might volunteer their services a few hours a week in drug addiction treatment centers. Contact with ex-addicts who are now working with addicts trying to kick the habit may act as a powerful deterrent to experimentation. Such concrete assistance and support would be very valuable to the clinics and hospitals engaged in the difficult and often thankless task of treating drug addicts. We believe that contact with alcoholics and lung cancer victims would also be helpful to students. The idea may at first seem shocking, but overprotection of our young from such harsh realities may assist them on the road to disaster. Drugs, formerly confined to high school and college students, have invaded the lower grades. Alcohol has become less a problem for older students since forbidden marijuana has come to the fore.

We believe the very first hint of a problem, even in a third grader, is cause for alarm. Teachers and administrators, resisting the easy cop-out of "protecting" the young from harsh realities, should plunge in with a full-scale discussion program in which the youngsters have a say about what they want to find out and how to attack the problem.

Most young people today are seeking a way to turn on, and are characteristically willing to work harder for what they want than grown-ups with the same purpose. But there are other ways to turn on, and better rules to be broken. The current encounter group movement, or sensitivity training, is concerned with ways of turning on without drugs, alcohol, or tobacco. Participants frequently report that they feel "high" after a few hours in an encounter group, perhaps because they are tampering with some of the social rules for living that are also weakened by drugs or alcohol, but are doing it with full awareness and a sense of adventure which adds to the zest.

We would encourage educators to experiment with other means of turning on. Encounter groups and sensory awareness experiences do not damage the liver or the psyche if conducted by a responsible and well-trained person. The courage to speak the truth and to seek new truth through responsible experimentation is the best help one can offer students attracted by drugs, alcohol and tobacco smoking.

FIGHTING

A visitor from outer space would find our world strange indeed. A fist fight or a wrestling match in school, capping stirred feelings, is enough to cause momentary panic in half the teachers and half the mothers in our country. Yet many of these same people support "justifiable" war, and calmly sip coffee before the television set watching a soldier being mortally wounded or a student demonstrator being clubbed on the head. Our children must get an unclear message, to say the least, about where we stand on fighting and other forms of violence.

To clarify our own position on this fundamental aspect of growing up, we would like a young child to feel sufficiently strong and aggressive to protect himself. Once that self-image is well under way, he should get the idea that striking someone as a means of expressing his inner feelings about that person is a babyish method that may not only cause physical hurt but also strain the relationship. We would like to help him, even at an early age, seek better means of expressing the same angry feelings.

When questions are asked about men hitting and killing one another, we have to admit that many men have not really grown up in some ways. They may never have grown-up ways to express anger or to settle a difference of opinion, or may sometimes get so carried away by their feelings that they strike out babyishly. Most children understand this through daily evidence of regressive behavior in themselves and others (for example, an older child who occasionally wets his pants or has a temper tantrum). They may be surprised that adults revert to infantile behavior at times, but soon realize that they do.

A subtle point is that many males in our culture try to show their manliness at moments when they feel least sure of it by resorting to physical violence. The quickest way to start a fight in a bar is to cast asperations on someone's manliness. To prove he's a hell of a fellow, he will have to fight. Obviously, if he were sure about his manliness he wouldn't have to prove it to himself or others.

These lessons hold more clout for growing boys than for growing girls, but are also important for girls, since many of them will be the mothers and teachers of future generations of men.

Part of a boy's confidence in his manliness, as mentioned earlier, is the feeling that he is physically strong and thus able to protect himself. We would like to see fight training offered in schools. Not the kind that merely establishes a pecking order (who is best), but a cooperative venture in which all try to help each other feel totally competent in the art of self-protection. That means a boy would be acclaimed not necessarily for his ability to beat anybody in the class, but for his ability to help a frail inept youngster develop his own style of self-protection. A great deal of retraining, involving self-examination by the personnel involved, would be needed before even a skeleton teaching force for fight training could be developed, but the dream may some day come true. When youngsters are helped to feel safe from physical attack, they are free to find better ways of expressing anger or settling differences with others. We would like to inculcate the idea of making peace with one another out of strength, not fear, knowing that peace is superior to war.

This leads, of course, to the mature understanding that a fight or a war cannot always be avoided. If attacked physically, one can try to settle the matter peaceably, but if all other means fail and his life is in danger, he may have to strike back. It would be wonderful for a whole generation to learn this, and that meeting violence with violence even when seemingly necessary, may engender guilt and remorse, as well as a vague suspicion that things might have been settled in some other way. There is room for consideration of the philosophical implications of pacifism. Youngsters like to play with such ideas as, "What would happen if a country declared war and all its citizens refused to fight?"

Fights in a classroom don't follow the same pattern, so our advice is to look closely at the kind that breaks out. It will help to have consulted your own feelings beforehand, whether you ever fought or still do, and enthusiastically or not. If you avoided fights in your school days, you'll find it difficult to understand the ones that pop up in your classroom. You will need to think about what fighting means, under what circumstances you disapprove of it, and whether you would fight for what you believe.

The Pseudo Fight. This kind of fight seems more like a display of awkward friendliness. Sometimes the fighters wear a tell-tale smile but a tough look may be a rule of the game. You may feel a little stupid but it often helps to ask if they are having fun. With a convincing "no" from either youngster, it often makes sense to suggest that they get on to something both can enjoy. If they are trying to settle a difference or express some feeling, this can be done in a way acceptable to both.

The Angry Fight. This kind of fight is designed to cause pain and vent angry feelings. Someone throws a toy, draws a knife, or grabs a handful of hair. The fighters must be restrained but that is only the first step. The class-community cannot depend upon a king or a policeman to control such impulses; control can come only from clear, strong, and active community disapproval. A policeman, one citizen doing his job, could stop the behavior for the moment, but the community leader must mobilize the citizens to hammer out some acceptable plan of prevention.

School years are a good time to learn how to control one's own impulses and to voice disapproval of the antisocial actions of other members of the community. If the offender is sent packing to the principal's office for punishment, the lessons being learned are poor ones, *e.g.*, "I'm too tough for my teacher to handle" and "the principal's job is to dish out punishment." Our orientation places the problem of angry fighting squarely upon the classroom community. Discussion is mandatory; it will take time but everyone is learning, and a life may be saved some years from now.

The Assertive Fight. The assertive fight may resemble a pseudo-fight or angry fight until one explores the circumstances that seemed to provoke it. A youngster says, "He called me a dirty Jew again so I socked him." Everyone has the right to protect his heritage, of course, but must come to see that his fist offers the least mature way of doing it. You do not want to see a student fight his way to the electric chair or a prison cell, nor do you want to turn a fighter into an obsequious yes man. The task is to help him learn to fight at times and in ways that win him greater respect from himself and his community. His fighting spirit might be enlisted to help a whining compliant classmate learn how to square off against life. If they could be involved in a close working relationship, one might lend the other courage while he himself received hints about how and when to use words instead of fists.

A youngster who today speaks with his fists can learn to rely more and more on intellectual weapons, but he must see each step of the substitution as safe and possible. If he feels stupid, fists probably seem safer to him. Perhaps you could help him win respect with words.

Fights are often based on fear. If you can reduce the fear level in your classroom, you will reduce the number and the destructiveness of the fights. Every time you help a student feel more confident and competent, you lesson his fear. In a dark alley, whistling helps, but you feel better when a friend is with you. A simple sociogram can give clues to help fearful youngsters find buddies. Relationships then can be abetted through seating arrangements and project groups.

The Inner-City Child. Fighting can represent something quite different to children growing up in various subcultures within our society. Those reared in the ghetto, the inner city, or the slum are often identified as culturally disadvantaged, culturally different, coming from a lower socio-economic class, minority group members, welfare recipients, or just plain *poor.* The wide variety of awkward terms represents an embarrassed attempt to deal with subcultural groups that continue to get the short end of the stick. They are indeed disadvantaged, one way or another.

Fighting among disadvantaged children may present special problems for the teacher. If a poor child is also a member of a minority group he has probably learned that the teacher and the policeman are not friendly authorities but "those in charge," that he'll have to take care of himself and seek his own justice, which can become a full-time job. The fight may interfere with your lesson plan but it can keep warm the youngster's flagging self-esteem, a more urgent matter than algebra at any given moment. It would be fine if he could protect his self-esteem and even increase it by learning algebra. He is sure to respond more to pressure from irate peers than from an irate teacher. But the peer pressure must come from the warm bodies of equals and not a few cold words of wisdom from the teacher's pets. This means real use of town meetings in the classroom and equal weight for every voice.

Even though a fist fight may be stopped by physical restraint or a loud command, we cannot pretend it did not happen. Everyone has seen it and is ready to learn something about why people fight and about the power of words. If the pen is not mightier than the sword, we teachers might as well close shop and put our money into guns. Education provides an awareness and mastery of emotion that puts us in an improved fighting position.

It is worthwhile for your students to think through why and how people fight, and decide when a fight is good or bad. They can learn alternate means of expressing and thereby releasing anger. They might take the United Nations as a sophisticated example. There is no sense in stating categorically that fighting is bad for they know this is not accepted as the whole truth in our culture. But the classroom community can be a friendly place where constructive fighting is accepted and each person is protected from harm by community-enforced rules as well as by his own physical strength and prowess.

HOMOSEXUALITY

A teacher is often concerned about a boy's feminine mannerisms or a girl's boyishness, and the question of present or future homosexuality begins to loom large. Before we tackle this complex topic, let us clear away some frequent misconceptions. Each of us is born with a need for sexual activity, though that need does not blossom fully until puberty. The style of sexual activity one can enjoy is learned during the years of growing up. Sexual relations between members of the same sex is accepted in some parts of the world, but the practice is discouraged in many cultures including our own. From what we know of normal human beings, if they were living in a nonrestrictive society, they would probably enjoy a wide variety of sexual experience, including contact with their own sex. Homosexuality is not a disease or the result of a genetic defect; it is a problem of the strong taboo in our culture, which makes some youngsters have an almost compulsive need to indulge in it. Homosexuality sometimes expresses a deep-seated psychological conflict. It may be a sign of other serious troubles considered sick, or it may be exploratory attempts to satisfy natural curiosity or simply a bold expression of affection.

The fact that homosexuality is more of a problem for boys than for girls has generated an enormous amount of research and speculation. Boys grow up in a female-dominated world; the mother rules the home and the female teacher rules the elementary school, although an increasing number of males entering elementary school teaching will hopefully change this picture. A young boy is pressured to learn to be a man but has little chance to study adult male models during the school day. He may also suspect it is not so wonderful to be a man who has to go to work each day while women wield the real power in the real world (kitchen and classroom). It is easy to see how this state of affairs may undermine a young boy's developing sexual identification as a man.

Furthermore, growing girls are permitted to hug, kiss, touch, hold hands, and brush each other's hair (behavior that in boys would cause comment) and also have more physical contact with both parents than do boys. Since a father usually begins to feel strange about hugging, kissing, and fondling his son at quite an early age, the boy may develop a kind of affectional hunger for physical contact especially with other boys and with adult males. He can pretend he does not want it and eventually divert this need so that it is met largely in affectional physical contact with females and some ritualized contact with males, as in body contact sports. As a result he is at a disadvantage compared with his sister.

In addition to the normally operating factors in a growing boy's environment, there may be special ones. His mother, or a series of female teachers who have their own needs because of problems with males, may take it out on him. They may seductively lure a boy, only to push him away with derisive laughter and scorn when he finally approaches. Or a mother may rob him of his masculinity by calling him pretty or her baby and trying to tie him firmly to her apron strings. We see loving mothers engaged in this apparently innocent behavior every day. Amazingly enough, many boys survive it with unimpaired masculine identity, but many are damaged and reach manhood with sexual identification that has an uncomfortable balance of feminine, masculine, and neuter facets.

Nightmarish suffering may result because of the strong taboo against homosexuality. Many grown men in our culture today who have seemingly established a "normal" heterosexual orientation entertain secret doubts about their masculinity and thus their psychological health or their worth as human beings. This is a sad state of affairs.

Signs of change are in the air. Homosexuality is more openly displayed, discussed, and accepted today than in the past. Today's under-thirties, far more than previous generations, accept many forms of deviance or individuality, and they will soon set the standard for our culture. Weakening of the taboo may alter the cultural expectations of the developing young male, solving much of the problem. If he can enjoy more give-and-take of physical affection, for instance, and if elementary schools succeed in employing more adult males for him to use as identification models, he may have no more acute a problem than do girls in our culture.

A girl who is fairly free to explore pseudo-homosexuality through tender physical contact with other girls rarely adopts an exclusively homosexual orientation unless she is expressing psychological conflicts she cannot deal with satisfactorily. If boys are eventually permitted the same degree of freedom, then probably only the ones needing a way to express seemingly insoluble psychological conflicts will become *exclusively* homosexual. Ironically enough, our fear of homosexuality with its attending taboos is pushing many boys toward an exclusively homosexual orientation. A man who feels secure about his masculine identity is free to express both heterosexual and homosexual desires.

Here is where you can be extremely helpful. You cannot buck the cultural taboo, no matter how enlightened you are, by permitting or encouraging wholesale physical expression of affection among boys, but you can permit or encourage what the traffic will comfortably bear. If one boy touches the face of another with a look of exploratory wonder or in thinly veiled horseplay, you can ignore it. If it is called to everyone's attention by another student, you can shrug and say, "So what?" or "Big deal!"

A male teacher will do more harm than good by getting into hugging and kissing contests with a boy student, but you can feel free to put your hand on his shoulder, pat his back, or playfully ruffle his hair when you're given clues that he likes physical contact.

Any teacher can find ways for boys and girls together and separately to have more physical contact. Little children with arms around one each other can be going to Funsville, and older youngsters can be blindfolded and try to identify classmates by feeling their hands and faces.

Physical contact need not be sexual or lead to sexuality, though people certainly do worse things to one another than making sexual love. Open discussion in the classroom can help youngsters to sort out some of these values for themselves as individuals and as representatives of the upcoming generation. Our culture can certainly stand repairs. Our very peculiar values and taboos are evident daily on television, where a growing child can see real people, as well as actors, killed and maimed before his very eyes. We accept this placidly. But if a man and a woman were seen in naked embrace or two men were to kiss each other on the mouth, millions of viewers would protest to the broadcaster. We seem to find it more acceptable for strangers to kill than to love one another. This is a symptom of a culture that can stand a few changes.

It is most important for a teacher to have a sophisticated perspective on homosexuality and what it represents in our culture, to avoid doing more harm than good by everyday, unthinking reactions. The majority of children go through a seemingly homosexual phase but, like the stuttering phase, outgrow it unless adults throw a spotlight on it and make it a real issue. Practically all teachers have a hang-up about homosexuality, over- or underreacting to it and perhaps harboring uncomfortable memories from their own childhood.

We believe that when an adolesent's discussion or behavior indicates discomfort about his developing sexual identification, it's time to get him to a psychological specialist. He has given a sign of trouble under the surface, and he is entitled to an accepting unshockable adult who can help him sort out his sexual desires. While a sexual fling with another male may be rewarding for an adolescent, homosexuality as an attempt to *solve* his psychological problems can only lead to more trouble. Whether a young person's problem in this regard appears to be big or small, we think it is imperative to get him to a qualified, unprejudiced counselor to help resolve doubts about his sexual identity.

Reference to homosexuality in the classroom can trigger a discussion that goes into one's need for tender physical affection from members of both sexes and also offers a continuous opportunity to define what it means to be a man or a woman. Let us hope our students can realize that a muscle man is not necessarily a strong person and a Playboy bunny is not necessarily feminine, womanly, or even sexy. We should be able to identify our most manly men and our most womanly women—needed for leadership tomorrow—and to recognize emotional and intellectual strength. A real man is not unreasonably afraid of another man; he does not run either from that man's empty threats or from his tender touch.

HYPERACTIVITY

Our history as a frontier nation partly explains our great dependence upon the *normal* or *average* for guidance as to what is acceptable. As a new nation we threw out many time-honored guidelines from older cultures and adopted our own, but the community need for definite standards has made us pay undue respect to the norm. What most people do must be all right, we feel, but we are wary of exceptional behavior, convinced that it must be unusually good or unusually bad instead of simply different. This cultural quirk causes many difficulties for youngsters in our schools.

Hyperactivity is one example of behavior that causes trouble because it does not fit the norm. Use of the term *hyperactive* to describe a youngster who moves around more than others of his age gives us away. We imply that *very* active is equivalent to *too* active, and are suspicious of all that moving about because most of our students don't do it.

Removing the value judgment involved, we see that some youngsters move around a great deal, for reasons that vary from one youngster to another. One reason is temperament, a mixture of his particular physiological and emotional styles that was determined by his biological inheritance and early learning experiences. We might say some youngsters are especially movement-oriented by nature, needing to move their bodies in space. We can help them learn to be less active but we are working against a basic ingredient of self. It may be necessary, but we are treading on sacred ground and should keep in mind that we are teaching conformity.

Another possible reason for hyperactivity is organic, or due to current body needs. This may or may not be pathological. The youngster may move his body a lot this year because of all the complex changes going on in his body chemistry. Something may or may not be wrong with it, requiring a physician's diagnosis and care. When a psychologist or physician speaks of an organic basis of hyperactivity, he usually means some kind of brain damage, but we use the term in the more inclusive sense of the body's real needs, which would, of course, include those resulting from organic brain damage.

One reason for all youngsters to have a routine physical examination is possible organic difficulties, and the physician should be fully informed about the youngster's very active classroom behavior if that gives him individual identity. With available medical care and drugs it is often possible to control the disharmony or disease, due to organic pathology, that is causing the hyperactivity.

Cultural reasons often lead to hyperactivity in the classroom. Generalizations in this area are usually fruitless, but youngsters with a lower socio-economic background certainly tend to be more bod-

ily active than their middle-class counterparts. The more a subculture rewards children for sitting still and living inside their heads,
the less active they are likely to be in the classroom. The more the
subculture rewards them for exploring their physical environment
and for nonverbal expression, the less likely they are to sit still in
the classroom.

Finally, there are emotional reasons for hyperactivity. A youngster overwhelmed by numerous problems is likely to appear itchy,
jumping from one activity to another and finding it hard to concentrate. You probably remember times when you felt too distracted
by your problems to pay attention to a lecture on some abstract
topic, so instead you simply took a walk to think things over. A
very mild example is the caricature of the expectant father pacing
the hospital corridors.

The emotional and organic bases of hyperactive behavior may
be revealed in a youngster's inability to concentrate on any activity,
even one involving bodily movement. He appears erratice because
he finds it very difficult to stay focused or tuned in on what is happening. Hyperactivity that is culturally and temperamentally determined can usually be identified by the youngster's ability to
stay with any pursuit permitting him to use his body actively.
A differential diagnosis is not that simple, but with these broad
categories you may decide whether a youngster has organic or
emotional problems that should be diagnosed by a physician or
psychologist. Even if he is receiving the recommended help from an
outside source, the teacher must come to terms with his hyperactivity in the classroom, as well as that arising from temperamental or
cultural factors.

Some day classrooms will be passé, hopefully, because our educational process will be marvelously geared to the students' individual and social needs. But for now we would like to offer a little
advice about handling hyperactivity in the classroom. A teacher can
do two things: use his own ingenuity in presenting the curriculum
in ways that permit varying amounts of body movement, or let
students use their collective ingenuity to find ways of studying
while using their bodies. For example, young ones can learn arithmetic by hopping from square to square, adding steps, subtracting
steps, or moving in a column of tens, hundreds, and thousands,
chalked on the floor. Geography can become three-dimensional

with continents painted on the floor, while space can be explored through large planet and star mobiles. Literature can be acted out in drama as well as read. Undoubtedly ways could even be devised to act out laws of chemistry or physics.

Few of us can sit still happily for long periods of time—a fact teachers often forget because they roam about the classroom from the start to the end of each exhausting day. An in-service course with sessions lasting several hours often reminds us of the torture of being glued to a wooden seat for more than half an hour. The younger the person, the more excruciating the agony. Toddlers move constantly, and adolescents usually find it hard to remain seated for an hour, indicating that hyperactivity is sometimes not "hyper," but just normal activity seen without perspective. Thirty-five nine-year-olds in action may resemble a snake pit to one tired teacher. It is wise to ask yourself now and then if the class schedule has sufficient allowance for activity.

No matter how much activity is permitted or even encouraged as part of the curriculum, a few youngsters will seem to need more. Most monitoring jobs are phony busy work; the students know it but compete for the jobs principally because of the opportunity to move about. If you offer enough means of meeting the activity needs of most of the classroom citizens, genuine required jobs that involve movement can be reserved for the few youngsters who need them. It is usually easier for one person to pass out paper or collect assignments; moving about among his peers gives a student the happy opportunity to serve his own special needs and those of the community at the same time.

ILLNESS

A student may be ill a great deal during the school year; someone in his family may have a serious or puzzling ailment; or you may be ill yourself. Illness visits every classroom. Our culture is fairly enlightened about the subject, but we still treat it gingerly and a fair share of superstition surrounds it.

The happy, productive student or teacher is usually physically healthy. If physically unhealthy, he has difficulty being happy and productive. Cause and effect may not apply here but a circular process seems to be operative. Being physically healthy does not guarantee that you will be happy and productive but does make it more probable, and the reverse is also likely.

Physicians are the first to admit how little is known about why most people get sick. Sometimes the cause is a "bug" that some people were exposed to and others were not. Of those exposed, some got sick and some did not. Why? We assume that their resistance was low, or high. The experienced physician and the experienced teacher share the hunch that resistance to illness is based not only on adequate nutrition and rest, but also on feeling good about oneself and one's world.

A teacher can do little to help students protect themselves from the infectious causes of illness except to recommend cleanliness, nutrition, and adequate sleep, but as the class-community leader, he can do a great deal to boost emotional resistance to illness. Every step to ensure the individuality of each citizen in the classroom, to honor his integrity, to respect and assist in his search for understanding and to make him feel needed and wanted contributes to his happiness and productivity and makes physical illness less likely.

Students try to understand illness and to peer through the veil of superstition surrounding it. Our problem as teachers is to help them explore the truth about why people develop various illnesses, how they are cured if this is possible, and what protective measures they can take.

Superstition is hard to fight, especially with young children. It may be a good thing to look for ways in which we unknowingly feed the superstition. A student may be told, "You're a pain in the neck" . . . "You give me a headache" . . . "You make me sick" . . . or "You're making me a nervous wreck." Teachers and others in this way suggest that if they become physically ill, the fault will lie elsewhere. Such a communication says in essence: "I'm going to make you magically responsible when I become ill; you'll then be punished by your own guilt."

We have found it far better for the learning process that a teacher handle his anger with a student directly by admitting to the feeling, pointing out the student's particular behavior that provoked it, and trying to work out with him some sort of solution. To perpetuate childish magical games of guilt can only worsen matters.

A child often believes that he gets sick because of something he has eaten but more often than not the reason turns out to be something his mother has expressly forbidden, or it may be related to a taboo activity such as masturbation. As teachers, we should beware of encouraging (even by tacit agreement) the search for causes in the wrong places. One may become sick from eating a forbidden food or even conceivably hurt himself by masturbating but it would be unlikely.

Sorting out the real causes of illness of his own or those close to him is of compelling interest for a youngster. His search can constitute good classroom learning if approached in the right manner, since very similar methods apply to finding answers to other questions in life. He is learning how to learn.

Finally, illness offers a genuine opportunity for classmates to experience compassion and see more closely how vulnerable and interdependent we all are. Most of the acceptable responses to someone else's illness are stylized expressions of sympathy and good wishes designed to chase away unseen demons and expiate any guilt of one's own. Students can be helped to think what they wish to say with a get-well card or a phone call. Maybe they want to say, "I miss you" . . . "I'm glad it's you and not me" . . . or "I'm afraid to come near you for fear I'll get sick, but I'm ashamed to be such a coward." Maybe they want to say, "You get sick too much and it makes me feel guilty for being healthy" . . . "I know what you're going through; you're strong enough to take it so I won't weaken you by slobbering all over you with sympathy" . . . or "I love you so much I worry about you all the time you're sick, and I don't want you to see me this way because it isn't worthy of you."

None of these complex messages can possibly be transmitted in a cute little card with the message, "Sorry to hear you're sick/Get well quick!" Students given a chance to sort out, in discussion, in conference, or in composition, what they are feeling about someone who is ill, begin to see what they want to tell the other person and why. They may still choose not to send the sick person the whole message but they can send a message that is wholly truthful and communicates something to him. Such an exercise not only teaches a student a lot about himself, his beliefs about illness, and his feelings for the other person, but also helps him learn how to express his truth—a large part of what going to school is supposed to do for a person.

We would suggest that the teacher help a youngster rip away veils of superstition and look for the reasons why he becomes ill, try to understand how he feels about someone else who is ill and send a truthful message, and understand our vulnerability and interdependence as human beings. He should realize that under no circumstances is he responsible for the teacher's illness. It may be superstition that happy and productive individuals are less likely to be ill but, if so, it is a harmless one.

LAZINESS

You are sure to have heard some teacher describe a student as lazy, and perhaps have done so yourself. It is a peculiar label because to some extent we are all lazy or none of us is lazy. Actually everyone is lazy sometimes and very peppy at other times. *Not* to do something requires a definite effort. There is no such thing as genuine inactivity this side of the grave. A daydreaming child is a busy child. It may be tempting to pretend that a student's low academic achievement is due to laziness, but this answer won't hold water.

Laziness, or why Sammy does not run, is a norm-dominated concept like hyperactivity. We assume that there is a normal amount of work, or a normal amount of motivation. And so there is, statistically. Statistics tell us about the average for a given population but not about the individuals comprising it.

If you think in terms of normative labels such as "lazy," it's a good idea to look inside yourself. Do you have an unexamined prejudice about leisure, for instance?

Many of us were raised to consider hard work a virtue, which is a philosophical assumption but not a fact. A good case could be made for the assumption that work robs most people of the opportunity to taste, examine, or enjoy life's pleasures. In a thousand years machines may do most of the work; our descendants will consider us deprived primitives who had to work because we lacked sophisticated machines and made ourselves feel better by looking on work as a virtue.

So before becoming deeply concerned about a student's apparent underproductivity, we might first do some soul-searching and then find out how he views it. His productivity level in the academic areas we are examining may seem entirely acceptable because of his subcultural learning or the personal philosophy he is developing. You may disagree, but it would be bad taste to rush in and tell him he is quite wrong and should embrace your cultural norms and individual philosophy.

However, if his seeming underproductivity poses a problem to him as well as to you, it is time to take a closer look. A discontented student's lack of productivity is usually aimed at something or somebody; it is a kind of sit-in or passive resistance. A perplexed parent may be supplying the motivation. Inactivity is one way of eliciting parental concern when other ways have failed. An overproductive teacher provides the answer in another case; the youngster may believe that only by wasting his brilliance can he kill the teacher's overpowering love.

A youngster who seems apathetic or lazy in all areas is playing a very difficult role. It is a desperate measure. Young people are interested in a great many things and must have strong reasons for appearing generally uninterested in everything. They may sense danger in being interested or may have found apathy the only useful weapon against a strong teacher or parent. Before a teacher can offer them a helping hand, he must be aware of the problem and that it may be damaging.

Again, the best help may consist of simply providing opportunities for expression, discussion, or confidence. If the youngster comes to the conclusion that he can't possibly solve the problem, it may be the time to suggest consultation with someone in the mental health profession who is experienced in untangling psychological knots.

One thing is sure: calling a student lazy only vents your own vexation, anger, or feeling of helplessness. It does not help the student involved. We would suggest that teachers strike the word *lazy* from their vocabulary and then try to find more useful explanations for student behavior.

PHYSICAL HANDICAPS

If a youngster has poor vision, is unable to walk, is missing an arm, or wears a hearing aid, we are likely to put him in a special category marked *handicapped*. Cruel? No, we do it for his own good. He can be given special help with others like him. How could anyone call such altruism cruel? *We* call it cruel to the handicapped youngster and to his so-called normal peers. We put all our first-class citizens, the ones supposedly not handicapped, into a larger category marked *normal* and then begin to subdivide them into good readers, college material, hot-lunch children, and so on. Such categories are harmful to them as well as to the ones excluded.

Once and for all, we must face the fact that we share this planet with all varieties of human beings. If we are ever going to achieve some sort of harmony we must stop the separatist attempts at homo-geneity. Harmony is impossible if everyone in the group sings the same note. If you grow up surrounded by people who sing only your note and then are turned loose in a world full of people singing different notes, you will have no idea how to establish harmony with them.

Of course a child who is missing an arm or leg needs special help, some of which must come each day from educational special-ists with particular experience in teaching the similarly handicapped. More than that, however, help must come from other children in the class.

What can you do to help someone who is handicapped?

1. Accept him as an individual, including his handicap.
2. Stand ready to offer help *when he wants it.*
3. Ask him to share his assets with you and help you when he can.
4. Let him know that his classmates and you, the teacher, all have handicaps to contend with, whether obvious or not.

These suggestions, of course, hold good for establishing any human relationships. Each of us has handicaps we could rank from most serious to least serious in our personal appraisal. Some of them are physical and thus usually visible to others, but the majority are not. Because of our handicaps we each need the special help and ac-ceptance of others. It is very worthwhile to learn this during the school years, but we educators make it very difficult by continually emphasizing differences. No matter what we say in our moralistic lectures, we convey an insidious message that it is vaguely shameful to be different.

A child's physical defect may accentuate his personality prob-lems. Crossed eyes, for example, can make him feel discouraged and anxious, reducing his desire and energy for struggling to compen-sate for his handicap. A child seriously crippled, as from polio, often becomes overly dependent, constantly clinging to the teacher or to a classmate. His parents, having been through their own personal hell, may be less able to cope with the handicap than is the teacher. In the classroom, the youngster can be encouraged to find an area in which he can excel. He can be discouraged from being overly dependent, and shown how others compensate for their various handicaps, thus maintaining their autonomy and integrity. He can also be referred to a consultant in the school system who has special knowledge about his particular disability.

There is a growing trend in private schools in metropolitan centers to abolish segregation of handicapped children. It seems reasonable to believe that in time public school systems will adopt the policy of teaching all children together, including those with poor motor control, acute hearing loss, poor vision, speech defects, or other handicaps. Asya, as a teenager, visited a large European center for physically handicapped children. The youngsters' ability to make the most of their unimpaired senses and abilities made a profound impression. Those who couldn't walk had highly developed manual skill; those with poor vision had very acute hearing and sense of touch. Their struggle with physical reality seemed to have resulted in a high level of courage and self-determination. It seems too bad that they were uncomfortable with their visitor, whose own discomfort may have been ill-concealed. We believe that the handicapped would be helped to deal with their daily problems by so-called normal children, and that both would gain valuable experience in accepting and being accepted through the learning years.

PREGNANCY OUT OF WEDLOCK

Out-of-wedlock pregnancy has a Victorian sound, but we don't know a simpler term that is as descriptive. A recent report from the Department of Health, Education and Welfare states that one-third of all firstborn children in the United States from 1964 through 1966 were conceived out of wedlock. Hasty marriages accounted for the fact that only one child out of seven was born to an unmarried mother during that period.

Young people today obviously enjoy a good deal of sexual freedom and exploration. With availability of The Pill and various contraceptive devices, we do not know the reason for the alarming increase in out-of-wedlock pregnancies among students. Information about the proper use of contraceptives is given in the newer sex education courses, but many schools are still reluctant to offer such courses lest they be accused of condoning or encouraging sexual license. Even so, we would like such information to be freely available to all students. (If you are going to drive, you might as well have the license.) Unwanted pregnancies mess up or ruin the lives of too many young people who are unprepared to deal with the attending problems.

If asked what we think of premarital sexual experience, we would give our opinions and clearly label them as such. The youngster may have to consider his parents' feelings as well as public opinion in establishing his own code of sexual ethics. An open search for guidelines and a working philosophy is vastly preferable to the public virtue and private vice standards many people look on as natural.

If young people have decided to experiment sexually and do not desire pregnancy, they had better know about sound contraceptive procedures. Birth control clinics in major cities make information available on contraceptive agents and devices. It is much easier to prevent than to terminate an undesired pregnancy, but even that information should be available from reliable medical sources. The school system and community have probably defined the limits of your professional freedom in dispensing sexual information. We recommend that you give out as much as the law allows.

Illegitimacy is a dreadful word that only further encumbers a youngster who has been affected by it in some way. We use the word here because in our culture it covers the complex of problems resulting from birth out of wedlock. We believe it is shameful, however, that any human being should feel illegitimate or unauthentic as a person simply because his biological parents did not have a particular legal or religious ceremony. We believe that educators should be unwilling to accept such a label. Every child is entitled to understand that he has, or once had, a father and a mother who made his conception possible.

This problem can pop out in many different ways. A young boy accidentally hit by a hastily discarded baseball bat calls the perpetrator a "rotten bastard." Illegitimacy is far from his mind but, unfortunately, the boy running to first base has recently begun to have suspicions about his missing father who, according to his mother, died before he was born. He carries his mother's maiden name; there have been some whispered innuendo in the neighborhood and he is putting two and two together. Whether the answer hidden secretly inside him is correct or not, he believes that he is illegitimate and has cause for shame.

A high-school girl who discovers she is pregnant is already up to her ears in difficulties. A classroom reference to illegitimacy makes her wonder whether a forced marriage or an abortion might be a good solution for her.

A fourth-grade boy looks a classmate straight in the eye during a tense fight for status and says loudly enough for others to hear, "Your mother got ten kids by ten different men and you ain't got no Daddy, no how!" The child may feel close to his mother and siblings, but how can he respond? Must he lie and say he does have a Daddy at home? Must he pretend to disown his family to avoid being hurt by association when they are maligned? Must he start a fight to divert attention from what he feels to be the awful truth? Or can he be helped to realize that this truth, like any other truth about the world around him, can be faced without loss of dignity?

It is hard to believe that truly educated persons would hold the circumstances of a youngster's birth against him, yet we have all met such teachers. They have a prejudice which they have not learned to question. Even if they deny it verbally their behavior will show clearly that they think less of the child whose parents were not married when he was born. Like so much human interchange, it would be funny if it were not tragic. The message the child gets is: "Be ashamed of yourself."

In the learning atmosphere of the classroom quite a different message might be transmitted through seemingly unimportant asides, smiles, frowns, statements, and discussion. Such complex, behind-the-scenes messages are listened to carefully by the youngsters. Our message would read: "You are you. You did not make the world or anyone in it. You are responsible for what you do *for*, *with*, or *to* other people and for what you do *for*, *with*, or *to* yourself. You are not responsible for what other people do. You will make mistakes and learn through them. Your dignity as a human being will be challenged only if you act contrary to what you believe to be right, true, and good. Your worth as a human being will be questioned only if you choose to act in ways threatening to the well-being of others."

The concept of illegitimacy may serve our society by clarifying property rights and exerting communal pressure leading to family responsibility for defenseless children, but it can do great harm when unleashed as an unquestioned prejudice in the classroom. It shares with other forms of prejudice the potential for insidious damage. Classroom discussion and the teacher's attitude can do a lot to minimize the harm.

PREJUDICE

Each classroom offers a splendid opportunity almost every day for a discussion of prejudice, and the lesson learned may foster the students' growth and add to their widening experience. Learning involving emotions requires lots and lots of discussion to discard some old patterns and permit new ones to develop. The lesson is simple though it takes a long time to learn: *to pre-judge someone is to hurt him and to cheat yourself.*

As soon as we begin to talk, we are taught to generalize and to attach labels—a useful verbal skill, but it robs us of precious human experience. It is useful to be able to call all variations of a certain red, pulpy vegetable *tomato*, and to call certain things growing in the garden *vegetables*, but because you've bitten into one rotten or green tomato, you don't look on all tomatoes with disfavor and exclude them from your diet. Even if you're not wild about vegetables in general, you probably find some of them delicious. Generalizations and labels often keep us from the joys of experiencing the subtle differences in people as well as things.

Haven't you attached labels to people, and many times heard others do so? Here are a few: *wop, nigger, kike, mick, spic, clam digger, wetback, honkie, redneck, wasp, bastard, problem child, cripple, retarded, fairy, dumb, disturbed, old, kraut, hick, egghead, chink, shrink,* and *foreigner*. The prejudice encapsulated in such labels gives them their sole meaning. If you recognize these labels, you are tuned in to, if not in sympathy with, the particular prejudice implied. When you hear an individual given a label, you see him *through* it, and the burden of proof is on him to show he is not like all the others in the same category. You miss the chance to encounter him as a unique human being and you hurt him too. By pigeonholing him before getting to know him, you make it hard or even impossible for him to act naturally.

Practically everyone has met with prejudice at one time or another, or even every day, and found it painful. Imagine walking into a room where someone you have never seen before says, "Oh, you're one of *those*, I see. That's a shame. Of course, you may be one of the *good* ones." What does that do to your insides? How do you feel about him? How do you feel about yourself?

Whether encountered in kindergarten or college, statements revealing prejudice should be challenged. In the teachers' room you may hear, "There's nothing I can do to help Josh with his reading. Of course, he's one of those bussed-in kids." The assumption that all bussed-in kids are alike shows prejudice; it gets between the teacher and the student. A teacher cannot see the student as an individual while classifying him as "one of those bussed-in kids."

Trying to catch one another in prejudicial statements, whether about people, objects or phenomena, can be turned into a worthwhile classroom sport. Prejudicial generalization is a sign of poor education. The educated person has learned to question and search; he does not assume that he already knows.

Answering a "why" question with a label is an example of prejudice: "Why do you suppose that girl is so flirtatious?" "She's Italian." "Why don't you date him?" "He lives in the development." "Why not share your book with her?" "She's black." "Why don't you look at this book?" "It's about history." Are there no warm days in winter and no cold days in summer? Prejudice blocks your intake of information and the use of your five senses and intelligence.

For years teachers have piously bombarded students with guidance lessons on the evils of prejudice (usually racial) because it hurts others. We suggest that everyone alive has some prejudices; the best we can hope for is to become sufficiently sensitive to our own to force them aside, permitting our senses and intelligence to take over. We can all become more adept at "catching" our own prejudices, especially if we enlist the aid of friends.

A teacher will get nowhere if he pretends to be free of this malady. He must invite the youngsters to help him guard against his own prejudices and hope they will tender him a similar invitation. Moralistic lectures go in one ear and out the other, as usual. Only through open classroom discussion can students begin to see that their prejudices not only hurt others but cheat themselves. The realization of self-cheating may eventually provide the motivation for unearthing prejudices and actively controlling them.

Discussion of this topic comes up again and again and again. A black youngster says, "I don't like white people." A black teacher replies, "I like being black too, but Peter is white and you like him, don't you?" "Yes." "Then how can you say you don't like white people?" "Cause they've done bad things to us." "Who is 'they'?" "The Man, Whitey, Mister Charley." "Is Peter 'The Man,' 'Whitey', or 'Mister Charley'?" "He's white." "But you like him." "Yes." "Has Peter done bad things to us?" "I don't think so." "If you hadn't grown up with Peter in this neighborhood, and you just happened to see him on the street, you'd notice he was white." "Yes." "And you wouldn't like him because he would be one of 'them'." "Right." "Then you'd miss out on a good friendship if you judged Peter before getting to know him."

It is terribly hard to sort out all of the feelings and drive home this lesson. The black boy cited above has been hurt by the prejudice of many white people. He is striking back and trying to find his identity, but will cheat himself if he is not careful. Prejudice often appears to exist for good or understandable reasons but it always holds this threat as well as perpetuating a vicious circle of human hurt and hatred.

A high school youngster says, "No history courses for me; I don't need them." His advisor says, "But you read everything you can find about President Kennedy." "That's not history. That's a person." "You admire him a lot but he's not alive any more. If you read about him or see a movie or TV program about him, you are studying history. If you had been born after President Kennedy's assassination and were determined not to study history, you never would have known anything about him. Yet might admire another man even more than President Kennedy, but you wouldn't even *know* about him unless you studied history." "But history is boring." "Perhaps your teachers and books so far have been boring, but you can look for the interesting ones. If you're prejudiced, deciding in advance that they're all boring, you'll never find out about an unknown man you might admire even more than President Kennedy. It is your choice. You may cheat yourself if you wish, but please be aware that you are doing it."

The civil rights revolution has brought home a good lesson. People are learning to take pride in their black skin, their Spanish heritage, or their foreign background. The revolt has spread so that we have seen poor people marching proudly and homosexuals picketing for legislative changes. The lesson in self-pride, a great gift to all of us, is continuing. As teachers, our problem now is to encourage class discussions in the hope of convincing a youngster that he cheats himself by generalizing, categorizing, and labeling.

SEX EDUCATION

Sex education is not a "problem," but it is a concern for many teachers today. Sex education, usually of the informal variety, has always been with us. Youngsters have greedily sought information, sensing the great importance of sex because we have shrouded it in secrecy and continually hinted at its mysteries. Each year more and more schools are introducing courses in sex education. There is an excellent chance that we will dampen the youngsters' natural interest in sex by droning on about ovulation, fertilization and other aspects that least concern them. Look what our schools have done to an interesting topic like mathematics! But perhaps the new generation of teachers will be less frightened by open discussion of sex, and therefore handle such discussions in ways that reveal their own interest and satisfy, rather than fend off, curiosity.

The current demand for sex education stems from the general upheaval of old sexual guidelines. The so-called sexual revolution has been reflected in communications media at a relatively sophisticated level. Since most children watch television daily, their curiosity is aroused at an early age. We need a substantial curriculum on sex covering very young children up to young adults, to counter this overemphasis on sex.

Obviously, a good deal of difficulty could be avoided if parents and teachers would join forces to broaden the child's understanding of physiological and anatomical matters from the earliest years. This is one of several ways of helping him develop a healthy respect for his own body and the bodies of members of the opposite sex. It is quite normal for a two-or four-year-old boy to show off his penis proudly or to try to explore little girls' bodies, but by the age of 10 or 12 he already knows how boys and girls feel and look and function, and doesn't yet need a sexual object for gratification. A teacher may be embarrassed to observe overt sexual play even by very young children; more importantly, and for reasons not yet well understood, other children become just as anxious on observing it.

Youngsters should be better able each year, from kindergarten into high school, to grasp what it means to be a man or a woman, the male and female roles in our society. Many parents and teachers fail to lend support during each particular phase of maturation because they are inhibited in regard to their own sexuality. If grownups find themselves confused by the flood of provocative sexual material loosed by television, radio, billboards, magazines and movies, how much more confused and bothered must youngsters be by the overstimulation?

There is no minimizing the difficulty of handling sex education effectively. We believe, however, that the growing child should receive sound information geared to his current needs so that he can integrate it gradually. Then by the time he reaches puberty he may have less trouble coping with his emerging strong emotions and body changes. His development of ego control and increasing ability to postpone immediate gratification also enter the picture at this time.

Little children are first interested in the basic mechanics of sex. Where do babies come from? How do the male and female seeds get together? How does Daddy get his penis into Mommy's vagina? Such questions put some adults up-tight, but they are just as valid from the child's viewpoint as other questions: What makes the automobile go? Where does the gasoline go after the man puts it into the tank? How does the gasoline make the wheels go around? Why do you have to insert the ignition key to make the car start? There are straightforward questions to elicit information that will broaden his understanding.

Later on the youngster begins to wonder why people want to have sexual intercourse or why they want to make the car go somewhere. In late adolescence, like a connoisseur, he begins to be interested in the erotic and exotic for its own sake. How does a man develop into an irresistible lover?

Sex is still very frightening to most educators; tons of colorless manuals and workbooks are being published to make sure the subject is taught in a mechanical, uniform, comprehensive fashion that makes it less and less interesting. Unfortunately, we may have to go through this stage before an emotionally laden topic can be fully introduced into our sterile curriculum. The prescribed courses of study vary considerably from one school system to another, but in general we have found it wise to answer questions as honestly as possible, sticking to the question asked, rather than basing a lecture on it.

Such an approach seems especially helpful in an area where your own emotional reactions make you feel unsure. Sex is related to, and in fact the core of, the whole wonderful topic of human existence. More than enough stimulus material is available on television, in newspapers and in everyday neighborhood happenings to make for easy discussions.

The teacher can offer still another kind of help traditionally restricted to the elementary grades—bringing the world of nature into the classroom in tangible form. We see no reason why it is not used to advantage at all levels of education. A third-grade teacher we know has an aquarium, birds, bunnies and hamsters in her classroom. With so much life demanding attention there are constant references to procreation, pregnancy, birth, illness, growth, and death. Paintings, drawings, poems, elective reading, anatomy and physiology, and even math lessons can be related to these themes. This rich background contributes to the kind of perspective that education aims to provide for children, and it is also a great experience for teachers who were reared in cities.

Sex education is a door newly opened in the formal curriculum. We may need to hang draperies in the doorway for a time, but hopefully we will soon be used to it and can take the children on a relaxed exploration of this basic life experience.

SEX PLAY

The present revolution or upheaval of accepted standards has come about rapidly. Some people are delighted with the changes; others are frightened or repelled. We believe that when the dust settles, the changes will definitely be for the better. People respond with changes in standards and attitudes when they can no longer stomach the old culture. Change comes because it has to come. A thousand years, and many other sexual revolutions, from now will find today's swinger a curious artifact. Meanwhile, we two authors have a problem: anything we say about sex may be outdated by the time it is published. For that reason our advice will be a little more abstract than usual.

First, let us admit that unless we have been taught to associate it with fear of revulsion, sex activity of any sort feels very good. Sex play between two or more youngsters feels good, too, and also permits them to learn about one another. If they are naive, they may compare notes about other bodies. Even well-informed youngsters have a chance to learn about another person who is part body and part abstractions, such as invisible organs and thoughts. Nursery school children commonly explore each other's bodies to indulge their healthy and natural urge to learn, an activity that may provoke anxiety in an adult who observes or learns about it.

The adult's mounting anxiety about sex exploration as youngsters grow older is due largely to feelings about his own controlled impulses, worry about what the principal or the neighbors would say, and about whether it might warp their sex life when they grow up. Actually, many adults probably have a warped sex life *because* of all those "don't look" and "don't touch" restrictions during childhood.

It is well to recognize that youngsters of the same age are not necessarily ready at the same time to cope with their own impulses or those of other youngsters toward them. Open sex play in the classroom, even some time before puberty, may create an atmosphere so sexually exciting and titillating that they become engulfed in voyeuristic and exhibitionistic interactions, building up body tensions to a high pitch. Since the tensions cannot readily be released, it is well-nigh impossible to maintain a suitable atmosphere for cognitive learning of any kind. Many teachers and parents will undoubtedly have to alter their outmoded views on standards of sexual behavior in our society. Who knows whether classrooms of the future will find nudity an aid to sex education?

The most constructive responses to sex play in this time of rapid change depend upon factual information. The teacher need not feel it his duty to reinforce social taboos; plenty of people in the outside world are doing that (and the taboos are also changing rapidly). However, he does need to develop a facility for quickly responding and answering truthfully as best he knows how.

How does a teacher react on discovering 10-year-old Johnny and Mary Jane exploring each other's bodies in the coat room? They may feel guilty but outwardly seem very pleased with themselves. If he is about to come out with an abrupt "Stop that!" he might first stop and ask himself why they should. If he fears that their parents will find out, be furious, and hold him responsible, that thought must be contained in the injunction. If he fears the other youngsters will follow suit, he must face why he does not want that to happen. The possibility that this highly charged emotion will be contagious and they will never get back to their lessons, or that the principal may walk into the room, will probably flash through his mind. A constructive teacher who has learned to tap his own feelings may say after a moment's pause, "I think you ought to stop that. You aren't going to feel good about it, and would probably be upset if your parents knew. Anyway, there isn't time now so let's get back to the lesson."

That rather two-dimensional picture is meant merely as an illustration. In depth and color, it would contain the teacher's feelings about both pupils, their feelings about him and each other, the classroom climate, and the current standards about sex play.

Masturbation is an activity that has never been clarified satisfactorily. First, let us try to distinguish between masturbation that involves stroking the penis or clitoris to arouse sexual feelings and eventually lead to orgasm, and the kind in which a child clutches, squeezes or presses his sexual equipment because he feels tense or needs to go to the toilet. They are related because they both involved manipulation and elicitation of the same erotic feelings, but are quite different in intent and in the full feeling experienced.

We consider masturbation of both varieties a normal but usually private activity, not something to be done in the classroom, on the street, or in Macy's window. The privacy restriction has to do with its being a highly personal activity, like urinating or defecating (in our culture). There is nothing wrong or harmful about masturbation.

So if a youngster is clutching, pressing, or squeezing, you might ask if he or she has to go to the bathroom. If the answer is negative, you might tactfully add that touching himself in that way is making some other people uncomfortable. If a youngster is engaged in the kind of masturbation that leads to orgasm, you might suggest that he find another place to do it, since it makes some people uneasy and distracts him and everyone else from the usual classroom activities.

Beware! The area of sex is still explosive in our culture. Times are changing fast and that only increases the explosiveness of the moment. A teacher must be very careful in considering his own feelings in sexual matters and cautious in expressing them. He must try to gauge what the community will tolerate in truth in this area.

If he pushes the community further than it can go at the moment he may be the target of all the pent-up frustrations and anger that attends a world which is changing faster than those over thirty can comfortably change. He may be surprised at the overreaction from parents to his far-out statements of truth, but the reactions can cost him his job. As in other touchy areas, he will have to figure out how to get his job of truth-seeking done without violating his own professional standards, but without alienating himself from his customers.

We might add that moralistic lectures at this point in our history are worse than a waste of time. No one will listen to you because they are on the trail of something new and they are not interested in hearing how it used to be from someone who is unwilling or unable to take the trip into tomorrow with them.

SHYNESS

When people describe a youngster as shy they usually mean he is so uncomfortably self-conscious that it is difficult or impossible for him to act spontaneously in any situation. He literally becomes "up-tight." Our aim as teachers is to help him become increasingly aware of and comfortable with himself. One's self-concept in large part mirrors one's environment. A highly critical classroom promotes self-consciousness but not self-awareness, whereas an accepting classroom promotes self-awareness but not self-consciousness. The teacher is the person most responsible for setting the tone or atmosphere of the classroom.

Needless to say, you can't flood the room with mental health by pushing a button marked *acceptance*. If you want to transmit this message, it's a good idea to start with yourself. The more you like and accept yourself, the more you can accept others without judgment or reservations. This may be a spare-time exercise or a major undertaking requiring psychotherapy. If you think a little effort will suffice, note whether you place minor judgments on others or demand that they conform to your idea of how they should behave. You accept another person when you respond to him in terms of his self-image. If he is doing his own thing (which may be entirely different from yours) you will feel fine about it if you accept him. If he seems to be ignoring guidelines for the person he wants to be, you may feel uncomfortable but can still accept him.

Acceptance means "I'll take you just as you are and want to be. If you run into snags while moving toward your goal they will hurt you, and hurt me to watch, because they'll hold you up on your journey." Judgmental non-acceptance means, "I can't take you as you are because you don't fit my picture of the way a person *should* be. If you would just change a few things that are out of line, I could begin to like you." This is a very different kettle of fish and usually tells a great deal about how fully you accept yourself. If your reservoir of self-acceptance is low, we heartily recommend any exercises you can think of to fill it. Having a hard time genuinely accepting oneself is a good reason to enter psychotherapy, which is likely to pay marvelous dividends for you and your future students.

An accepting aura in the classroom extends to everyone. If Mark says something that makes Joey even more self-conscious, such as, "Hey, you need a haircut, Boy," he is after all doing his own thing. You might say, without sarcasm, "That probably won't help Joey enjoy his day very much, Mark."

Try to avoid having a self-conscious youngster stand in front of the class where all eyes are on him and all ears listening. If he does not yet have a reservoir of self-acceptance, this can be indescribably painful. You can let him know quietly and unobtrusively that you are aware of his presence and pleased to have him. This can be done with a glance, a smile, or a hand on the shoulder now and then. Your patience and effort will be repaid slowly but surely by his increasing trust of the class and of you.

Opportunities usually arise during the school year for a general discussion on self-consciousness. You may even contribute by mentioning a few things that have made you feel self-conscious. Such a discussion can be a real eye-opener for a shy child who has looked on this as his exclusive hang-up, who felt that he alone suffered discomfort when all eyes were upon him.

SPEECH DIFFICULTIES

A person is often compared to a walking millipede. He gets along fine until he pays attention to what he is doing and then he stumbles. Speech difficulties are very common in children between the ages of two and five years. We prefer to think of such difficulties in terms of "non-fluency" or "repetition of syllables" rather than "stuttering." It is all too easy for a child to be branded as a stutterer, which does not help him or help you to understand his problem. Besides, it is an oversimplification to lump various speech difficulties into one imprecise category.

Almost all of us have a momentary speech difficulty of some kind every week of our lives if not oftener. We ignore it because we are confident that it will pass; it does, and our usual speech patterns prevail. The worst thing that can happen to a youngster with a real speech difficulty is to have the teacher or the other students hang on his words. If he stutters noticeably, for instance, chances are that he is already very self-conscious. Our advice offered under "Shyness" may be useful here.

A youngster with a noticeable, persisting speech difficulty should have the help of a speech therapist. If none is available through the school system, the parents may seek help elsewhere. Syllable repetition usually has little or nothing to do with hearing deficiency and other organic factors. A quick test is to notice whether a profound stutterer can sing a song or tell a peer to go to hell without stuttering. If he can, the difficulty very likely has an emotional rather than an organic basis. However, professional assistance is advisable, since any speech problem other than syllable repetition may be complex and involve some organic malformation or hearing impairment. When no expert speech therapist is available, the teacher may find these guidelines useful in handling the youngster who only occasionally repeats syllables:

1. Discourage others from paying attention to his manner of speaking.
2. Do not pressure him to speak on his feet either at his seat or in front of the class. He will let you know when he is ready to give it a try.
3. Provide him with alternate attractive means of communicating and participating in the learning situation (writing being the most obvious example).

If the youngster can communicate comfortably in small group projects or through writing, and if the classroom atmosphere reduces his self-consciousness, his speech difficulty may be ameliorated to some extent. Like many problems mentioned in this chapter, speech difficulties may be rooted outside of the school. But since the student spends a great percentage of his waking hours in the classroom, a good experience there can help him sink new roots and come to grips with his problem.

STEALING

We are not the first, and will not be the last, authors to point out that our culture *pretends* to value people more than property but *acts* as if property is the more valuable. This double message causes endless confusion for growing youngsters. Taking someone else's property is considered legally wrong under almost all circumstances. The thief is caught and punished, supposedly to teach him not to steal again. The key words, *thief, caught, punished, steal* all have a negative emotional loading. Strangely enough, the thief's dose of supposedly re-educational punishment is heavier when the stolen property cannot be returned intact. If we were primarily interested in re-education, the punishment would be the same whether or not the property was recovered. The hidden truth is that we are primarily interested in the property; punishment is revenge for the thief and a warning to future offenders. This conflict in actual and stated values emerges clearly when something is stolen in the classroom.

Every teacher knows the moment when a terrified Susie says that Albert took a quarter from her desk, or a laughing Jimmy says someone took his condoms, or a surprised Cynthia discovers that her library book is missing. What can you do? You can, of course, say, "My job is teaching, not looking after your possessions," but that would be a cop-out. Your job is to help students learn what they need to learn; if you don't face the stealing episode you are ducking your responsibility. Stealing is such a hot issue in our culture that the concerned parties may be far too involved emotionally to pay attention to the lesson going on. This may also be true of the interested bystanders, so if you try to postpone the discussion very few students will have their minds on the lesson.

Meeting the emotional demands of the moment by rolling up your sleeves and going to work like a combined detective-policeman-judge is likely to provide more entertainment than learning experience. Stealing is a hot issue for the teacher as well as the students; your professional procedures may be blocked by your emotional reactions. Think of how you approach other less-loaded incidents of the day. If you are not sure how to begin, a discussion never hurts. Students begin thinking and talking about why it happened. (Why do people take things that do not belong to them?) Their emotional responses to stealing may keep them from looking for reasons. Out for blood and eager to explore the specifics of this case, they may all turn on Albert, who took something from a classmate several months ago.

The scapegoat is an interesting phenomenon that should be brought to the attention of all students. Albert or anyone else becomes a scapegoat partly because he is relatively defenseless and believes himself generally inferior or guilty, and partly because he is the handiest person on whom other members of the community can unload their own guilt feelings and thus appear virtuous.

When a student appears to be made a scapegoat, the teacher may say something like, "As a member of this classroom community, I can't stand by and watch this happen. Let's sit down together right now and figure out what's being done and why."

The teacher would also do well to keep a wary eye on the organization of a trial by students. Although a mock trial can be a very good way for them to learn the basic ingredients of civil rights and justice in a democracy, they may be tempted to turn it into a sordid game of power and revenge with each one waiting his turn to be judge so he can strike back at old enemies.

In such a situation, the teacher may insist that before the community becomes involved in the excitement of detective work or a trial, the members must try to understand something about property rights as well as civil rights within the classroom community. But patience! Growing up takes a long time; the youngsters will need many discussions before they are able to set adequate and fair community rules, and side paths must be explored meanwhile. Try to remember to ask more than you tell. Your students already grasp the usual concepts of right and wrong but they are now trying to broaden their personal understanding through first-hand experiences.

It may be hard for you to think this through for yourself. Our culture has strong, complex, and often unclear rules about property rights. When did you last take something that did not belong to you? Where was it? Were you in a hotel or a friend's home? Why does it seem more acceptable in a hotel than in a friend's home? Why do some people tend to take things more often than others? Why are some people robbed more often than others?

A teacher is in an especially good position to help students learn that people steal for many different reasons, for example, to acquire symbolic strength when feeling weak; to express anger by depriving someone else of his possession; to have something belonging to a person he loves or admires, in an effort to feel closer to that person. You can also help students think through why someone is considered innocent until proven guilty in a democracy, and why Shakespeare in *Othello* has Iago describe the theft of his purse as nothing, "but he that filches from me my good name/Robs me of that which not enriches him/And makes me poor indeed."

The long and the short of this is that the teacher's job would seem to be not to apprehend, try, and judge the thief, but to make opportunities for the class to talk about why people take things that don't belong to them and why a community must have ground rules that everyone is willing to follow and enforce.

Teachers frequently wonder whether it would not be better and easier simply to replace the missing quarter. It would undoubtedly be easier to replace it but you would be teaching your students to depend upon divine intervention instead of facing up to their community responsibilities. The loss of a quarter to buy a loaf of bread could be a tragedy to a child from a very poor family. But ten years later it would be far more tragic if all these youngsters had not learned to feel and accept responsibility for controlling stealing in their communities. Each person cannot guard his belongings every moment of the day. Responsibility must be cooperative. Community feeling should make it difficult to break the ground rules.

When Jimmy announces the theft of his condoms, the problem is to assure him you all know he is there and consider him a valued member of the community, so he doesn't have to play the clown to try to gain attention by shock tactics. When the quarter or the wallet is missing, the community's choice is between responsibility for setting and maintaining a fair set of ground rules and the harsh laws of the jungle.

SWEARING, CURSING, AND OBSCENITY

The difference between these three categories of words is obscure, at best, in regard to everyday classroom usage. Every teacher knows that so-called forbidden words are inevitable from time to time and cause a problem of sorts. As usual, before deciding what to do, it may be well to understand what is behind their use.

A teacher is often offended when a youngster usus an off-color word that he himself uses at times. We too often project adult meaning into a child's vocabulary. A teacher may be indignant if asked how to spell a forbidden word, yet the youngster who learns to spell it correctly is that much ahead.

We are aware that some communities and school boards consider that teachers are not quite human and should not use forbidden words or even admit to knowing them. The attitude can challenge the teacher's professional responsibility and threaten his financial security. The newspapers have carried stories about teachers who were fired, suspended, and/or sued for pronouncing such words in the classroom or writing them on the blackboard. In our culture, we still prefer truth in comfortable doses. If the community and school board or school administrators limit a teacher's academic freedom and he accepts this limitation, he will have to clarify this point for his students so they can understand the handicap they face in searching out the truth.

Language is the crucial key to communication and therefore possibly the most important skill to be developed during one's education. If children get the notion that some words are fun but other words are used in school, they will certainly not concentrate on the school-type words. We would suggest letting our eager young customers know that we consider words extremely important and will help them find out about any word that comes up. In the unlikely event that the teacher has never heard it before, other resource persons or reference books can be consulted.

Forbidden words are most often used to shock or to express a strong emotion such as anger. Profanity, obscenity, or cursing, when used well, can be most effective. Most of us have resorted to them, or wanted to, now and then. It is complicated to learn about when such words are likely to bring punishment, when the repercussions will be great, and when the words accomplish something worth the risk. The rare person who discovers forbidden words as an adult usually feels cheated out of some vital learning available to all the other kids during childhood. He resents the lack of early opportunities to develop a satisfying vocabulary, used or unused, of such words.

Almost all boys greatly resent teasing about being girls. (Some grown men feel the same way about subtle slurs on their manhood.) The teacher who overhears such a remark about Jimmy is more likely to be amused than upset, but he may register strong disapproval if Jimmy tells his tormentor to go to hell or to do something sexual with himself. If Jimmy does not already understand why the teacher disapproves, this is a good chance for him to learn, and any other interested students may as well be included in the discussion. The teacher may not be fully aware of why he reacted so strongly, and the discussion can help him find out. The assumption at first may be that he is upset because "I never realized that you were that kind of boy," but later it develops that in our culture forbidden words between children and grown-ups are taboo, while they're acceptable in the respective peer groups. According to this taboo, a "social inferior" who swears in your presence is insulting you by acting as if he were your social equal. You were probably upset because the boy subtly challenged your presumed superior status.

If a discussion about forbidden words is handled with sincerity, youngsters will very rarely carry home reports that set their parents on the warpath. If parents do storm in, charging you with using dirty words, you will have to explain that far from offering lessons in obscenity you were trying to help the students differentiate obscenity from other forms of language, and that you did not first introduce the words in the classroom. If pressed, you might even point out that parents, the principal, and almost all other adults know what the words mean, and to discuss them in an educational context seems more reasonable than to giggle about them in semi-secret through the years ahead.

If forbidden words enter the classroom as part of the student's normal expressive vocabulary, it is questionable whether they should be frowned on. The appropriateness of language is relative. Slum-reared youngsters usually have an infinitely more colorful vocabulary than well-to-do children. It is not an either-or thing, since the so-called privileged children can come out with shockers too. The point is that we usually forbid a slum child's use of a natural part of his vocabulary and at the same time keep a middle-class child from learning potentially useful language.

Why is language appropriate to a neighborhood not appropriate to the classrooms of its schools? Actually we are all further ahead if we can speak different dialects in any language. The person who speaks and understands many English dialects can communicate more easily than the person familiar with only proper English. Children with a colorful neighborhood vocabulary should not be shamed into believing that it results in poor communication. Their dialect is appropriate for one situation and proper classroom English for another. More and more heterogeneous peoples are found in schools, communities, and places of business. If one of the main educational aims is to prepare youngsters for participation in life, improving their tools of communication can undoubtedly be a big contributing factor.

Youngsters usually need a great deal of discussion and research to figure out the dialect appropriate for different situations. It is obviously as ludicrous to use college professor's English in a longshoreman's bar as it is to use ghetto language when applying for a white-collar job. It is incorrect, if not foolish, to consider one dialect better than another at all times; you will be fortunate if youngsters learn in the classroom that every dialect is correct in some situations.

If someone uses forbidden words to communicate surprise or anger you can let him know that the message is received. If the aim is to shock, the "cure" is not to be shocked, as any kindergarten teacher will testify.

TEASING

"I see London, I see France, I see Linda's underpants."

"All the other girls are invited to my birthday party—but not you!"

"You stink!"

"Hey, Tony, I hear you suck the teacher!"

"Look at the ring Jamie gave me. You're the last one left to find a man, Sally!"

The tone, style, and vocabulary change with the age and setting, but teasing is almost always an act of hostile aggression. It may be difficult to stop unless you can help to immunize the one on the receiving end. There is no fun in teasing unless it provokes a reaction. The victim is chosen with care because if the arrow is correctly placed there will be a satisfying reaction.

Immunity can be developed with a little time and effort, including a classroom discussion of the dynamics of teasing. "Why do you suppose someone gets a kick out of teasing people?" The teaser begins to lose his glamor; he may be considered an acute diagnostician of other people's woes, but is also seen to thrive on their misfortunes. With loss of his glamor is a concomitant loss of some of his potential for hurting. When such discussions are most successful, the victim comes to feel sorry for the teaser, who unfortunately finds this activity his best way of getting attention. The victim may turn from the teaser who is embarrassed by the display of his emotional poverty, or he may even try to be reassuring, *e.g.*, "You don't have to be like that. We could notice you and like you if you would just be yourself." If that message is sent with conviction, imagine the deflation of the teaser's balloon. He will undoubtedly try a few more times, but when he sees that his peers are onto his game he will slink harmlessly away. The problem may become one of helping him instead of trying to stop his annoying behavior.

Of course the discussion is not always that successful. He may have a perfect victim with an all-too-accessible raw spot. For example, he may go to work on an impoverished youngster who is deeply ashamed of his poverty: "Hey, man, where'd you get them fancy shoes? They got holes on the top and on the bottom too!"

If the class has had some discussions of teasing, and you sense that the poor boy is too damaged to rally and develop immunity against this form of assault, you may have to step in. "Look, Joe, I don't like the way you're hurting Emilio and I don't intend to stand by and smile. You wouldn't like it one bit if we all lined up and aimed for what we guess is your sorest spot. Please cut it out. I'm sorry you have to get attention this way. Until you can find better ways than baiting people I won't be a silent party to your unpleasant game."

If the shots are called honestly, other members of the class will undoubtedly support you. Beware, however, when the victim is someone you are not too fond of yourself; you may be dismayed to realize you're getting some vicarious pleasure from the sport. If so, it is a very good time to let your prefessionalism take the upper hand. Teasing is mean, regardless of the victim, and every effort should be made to stop it, for his sake and also for the sake of the teaser.

Sometimes you may overreact to some mild teasing that the victim can probably handle on his own. Seemingly inappropriate anger or other feelings may indicate the revival of something from your own childhood days.

One teacher in a teachers' workshop described a boy who untied the girls' hair ribbons and made faces at them. She found herself unreasonably upset and repeatedly warned him to stop. After several class discussions about teasing she realized that she was the only one genuinely bothered by his behavior. The girls pretended to be annoyed but gave themselves away with little smiles. It turned out that the teacher herself was the victim, though the teaser never approached her directly. When asked in the workshop to recall her experiences with teasing as a little girl, she said, "My God, my brother! What a menace. He teased me all the time, and I absolutely hated it. Now that I think of it, I'm not so bothered when a girl does the teasing in class but get in a tizzy when it's a little boy, especially if he's teasing a girl." This recollection made it easier for the teacher to see that she was reliving her own childish antipathy vicariously. She also began to realize that some cases of classroom teasing were far more serious than that of the boy who had bothered her most. As her disturbance with it receded, she noted that his behavior began to disappear.

You cannot successfully defend the target of teasing but you can help to immunize him and render the teaser impotent. If that fails, you have the right to call the shots truthfully on the dynamics of teasing. In the unlikely event that all of these means and the class discussions fail, you may have to sit down with the teaser and victims and say that you yourself find the situation too upsetting to be tolerated any longer. If they can't resolve the problem you will have to suggest that the teaser be transferred to another room where the teacher may be better able to help him.

If you resort to this last step before trying all alternatives everyone will see it as a cop-out, ignoring any psychological explanation you may offer. It should be used only when you are willing to admit to the teaser and the others that you have honestly tried everything you can think of without success. That is sometimes a turning point. Someone else may have an idea that saves the day or the offender, perhaps genuinely touched by your attempts to help and your honest admission of failure, may put in the extra effort needed to solve the problem.

TENSION

The problem of tension can be encountered because of a so-called nervous or high-strung youngster, or because you are aware of your own uncomfortable tension, or because you sense a general air of tension in the classroom. If life followed television commercials, the obvious solution would be to take some sort of pill. Yet most of us realize that a pill is more likely to dull our awareness of tension than to relieve the tension itself.

One of the antidotes for tension is emotional release in an atmosphere of acceptance and reassurance. Some people can best release a lot of tension by screaming, laughing, yelling, crying, hitting something, or jumping up and down. Unfortunately, our schools seldom provide adequate opportunity for this kind of behavior. It's a hope for the future, but for now we must find ways to work within the existing framework.

We have spoken earlier of establishing an accepting atmosphere in the classroom, which we consider the most important contribution a teacher can make toward relieving tension. A youngster or a teacher who feels he is on trial or being judged only becomes more tense.

There are many symptoms of tension, among them nail biting, constant body scratching, pulling at one's own hair, pressing the genital areas, and various facial tics. Any teacher finds these symptoms distracting when he is trying to get on with the learning business. It takes noble restraint to keep from saying, "Stop that!" even if you know the command will be ignored. When discharging tension in some way (perhaps wiggling a foot of a crossed leg), we all know it does not help to have someone tell you to stop. At best it makes you momentarily annoyed at him and you will return to the foot-wiggling as soon as your thoughts are again distracted. At worst, it builds up the tension further.

Fortunately, schools offer physical education classes which, under a thoughtful instructor, often allow for considerable discharge of tension. Less aware instructors erroneously believe a good rollicking game of dodge ball relieves tension all around, but it may actually increase the tension of the youngsters who are nervous about hitting and being hit.

It sometimes happens that you are on good terms with yourself and generally accepting of others but a shy, self-conscious youngster in your class seems to rub you the wrong way. If this is the case, we suggest examining your feelings and associations regarding him. Do you have any bones to pick with him? How does he annoy you? Would the same behavior from another youngster be equally annoying? Do you nag him sometimes? Maybe you can curb the nagging, but the pressure is likely to continue until you understand why he "bugs" you so easily. Perhaps he reminds you of your earlier self or some part of your present self. This sort of insight may help you to remember that he is himself, an entity not related to any part of you. It might even help to discuss the problem with him if you can manage to focus on yourself and *your* particular behavior toward *him* instead of the other way around.

Assuming that you do not have any unusual feelings toward a self-conscious child and still find his self-consciousness striking, its roots may well lie almost entirely outside of the classroom. If this is true, a good classroom experience during this school year can help him to sink new roots in healthier soil. Many a self-conscious youngster has begun to develop confident self-awareness in an accepting class with an accepting teacher. The usual academic skills can also be used to advantage. One can, as part of school work, talk about, write about, read about, or even act out in role-play, things similar to those causing individual tension. In an accepting atmosphere there is ample opportunity to find the right kind of activities to lessen the tension.

If a youngster appears to be growing more tense despite your efforts, it might be a good idea to examine your relationship with him. Whatever is going on at home or in the outside world, he should show signs of lessening tension in the classroom setting if he senses an accepting atmosphere. If you do not find any particularly negative feelings about this youngster, you might tell him you are concerned because he seems uneasy. The conference might not go anywhere because you can only tell him how you feel and hope he will be able to do the same. Sometimes the conference appears useless but the next day the youngster begins to show positive signs of change. You may never know why. Maybe he needed to know you cared, or maybe you could simply see him more clearly. If things do not go better, you can only keep trying and hoping. It might be fun to have your whole class suggest ways of releasing tension as a group without risking reprisals from the school establishment.

TICS

A tic, sometimes referred to as a nervous twitch, may be a rhythmic facial squinting, the twitching of one shoulder, a repetitive jerking of the head, or any number of other body mannerisms. Whatever its form, a tic must be considered a very special danger sign in a youngster. His parents should be strongly encouraged to seek psychological help for him, if at all possible. A tic has deep emotional roots. The youngster is telling the world that his inner emotional conflicts can no longer be contained and are bubbling to the surface.

Actually you may have clues to the roots of a tic. One youngster's tic consists of periodically shutting his eyes very tightly as if his body is telling him not to see. Another's tic is a caricature of a nervous smile, the kind donned by someone frightened or ill-at-ease who is trying to appease a threatening person. But this is definitely not the place for amateur psychotherapy. No matter how sensitive you are to the message sent out by the youngster's body, keep your insights to yourself and try to get professional help for him.

If such expert help is absolutely unavailable, a few first-aid procedures may alleviate the pressure until the youngster can be seen by a psychotherapist. They consist of creating opportunities for him to drain off excess feelings, such as assignments with plenty of leeway: writing short stories, poetry, fictional newspaper accounts, horror stories, or science fiction. The less articulate youngster may find painting, drawing, clay modeling, mobiles, collage, montage, or papier-maché work helpful. If movement-oriented, he may welcome the opportunity to run, do creative dance, or dramatic pantomime in which he fights off hordes of imagined enemies.

Excess emotion can also be drained off in class discussions. Youngsters can focus on contemporary celebrities, historical figures or literary characters, pointing out their motivations and feelings, also bringing in first-hand experiences and feelings if they wish to do so.

All these means enable the youngster to express hidden conflicts and the excessive feelings attending them. He will not really be helped to solve his problems, but some of the pressure may be lifted. In dramatic role-play, for instance, he may express deep hatred and murderous anger about someone and a moment later express very tender feelings of love for the same person. The class discussion may allow us to understand and accept this universal ambivalence illustrated in seemingly conflicting feelings for the same person at the same time. The students may begin to look on love and hate as two ways of expressing a great deal of care for someone, not as opposites. The opposite of both love and hate is indifference. Even if the discussion is focused on some mythological or fictional dramatic character, bringing out into the open the universality of love-hate feelings helps to reduce the youngster's tensions.

If a tic rapidly becomes habitual and attracts attention from peers, the teacher may wish to say casually, "Yes, I've noticed Mary Lou's squinting but haven't paid much attention to it. All of us have funny little habits from time to time. If I were in Mary Lou's shoes now I'd appreciate your disregarding my squinting as much as you can."

A little "magic" may work with a very young child when non-verbal experiences such as clay modeling, painting, and dramatic play do not seem to do the trick. Very often the tic is expressing a conflict comprising anger and fear of "letting it out" because of possible retaliation. For example, you can give a four-year-old a magic penny to use in a special make-believe way. "If you rub your thumb on the side where the head is, you can pretend to make someone disappear. If you're mad or want to get rid of him for some other reason, make him disappear quick as a wink. Then, if you change your mind, just turn the magic penny over and rub your thumb on the other side and pretend to make him come back. It's fun. Here, take the penny and rub the head side and pretend to make me disappear." (Child rubs penny.) "See, I'm not here. Now rub the other side and make me come back." (Child complies.) "See, here I am again. Why don't you keep the penny handy and use it to make believe you can get rid of someone you're mad at? When you feel like having the person around again, just rub the other side of the penny."

With this kind of first aid the tic may become less marked or even seem to disappear. But it is simply a stop-gap measure until the youngster gets some professional help. The symptom becomes less apparent with removal of the pressure but the inner conflicts are still there and the youngster has sent a clear message that he may be unable to handle them alone.

VENEREAL DISEASE

We also believe youngsters should be told that physicians treat venereal diseases and any other disorders without tattling to parents.

If venereal infection is even suspected, they can seek medical advice with peace of mind.

According to a survey by the American Social Health Association in 1969, physicians unfortunately report to public health authorities only one out of every nine cases of gonorrhea treated. The infection sources of the other eight cases presumably remain untreated and free to go on infecting others. It is especially important to an infant's well-being for pregnant women to seek treatment at the first suspicion of venereal symptoms to avoid harmful effects on the infant she carries.

If our culture were not so phobic about sex we might by now have developed vaccines to combat VD. Many people feel that it is appropriate punishment for sinful behavior.

From a professional's standpoint, disease does not help anyone, nor does suffering with guilt, shame and fear. VD can be easily cured and should receive prompt medical attention with no complicating fuss.

WETTING AND SOILING

Lack of bladder and bowel control is often encountered in nursery school but rarely in high school. The older the youngster, the more likely it is that such lack of control represents a psychological difficulty. Even a high school student can have such an accident, but if he has more than one in a school year it would be worthwhile to find out why.

In our culture, urine and feces are considered disgusting. We learned to think of them as smelling bad. Because they are "rotten," "vile," or "shameful," they represent something vaguely wrong about the insides of our bodies. We usually close or lock the bathroom door so that others won't witness our shame or be offended by this disgusting expression of our inner bodies.

We are exaggerating slightly to illustrate the emotional message conveyed to a youngster who is learning about himself and the world he lives in. If all things coming from within our bodies (including blood, ear wax and nose-picking) are similarly unpleasant, shameful, dirty, or disgusting, then our inner bodies are obviously the same. We fool the world with a clean and acceptable exterior while hiding our vile unacceptable inner selves. If we want children of future generations to grow up with a good self-concept and pride in their human condition, we had better alter this course.

When a little one wets or soils his pants, a teacher should be matter-of-fact about helping him into fresh clothing rather than making a face or saying "ugh" to the odor. A cheerful attitude may require some retraining. It may help if you can convince yourself that the odor of the feces is not necessarily unpleasant, though we have learned to make this association. Most parents remember that a baby has to *learn* to think of his fecal odors as unpleasant; in fact, he may have discovered, to his joy, that feces offer a fine substitute for paint. Although his sense of smell is quite keen, he is an accepting soul and only gradually learns to place negative value judgments on his sensory information.

If you would like to help students feel good about themselves *in toto*, you might start by viewing their bodies (internal and external) as a pleasant miracle of creation. As noted earlier, the culture in which you have been trained implies a disgusting interior to human bodies, so be patient with yourself during a retraining period. It may help you and the students to discuss feelings associated with the insides and outsides of bodies.

Repeated wetting or soiling, even among fairly young children, usually indicates tension. Jane says, "I forgot to go to the bathroom." The teacher says, "It's all right. Let's find some dry clothes, though, to make you comfortable."

Children are usually secretive about wetting and soiling because they are ashamed. Classmates may tattle on them or tease them. Sometimes a puddle or the odor of feces gives them away. It is good to be able to communicate acceptance of this lack of bodily control. Left to their own devices in an accepting atmosphere, children often compare notes on such accidents and how they felt about them at the time.

It may help to remind a very young daily wetter to go to the toilet a few times during the course of the school day. If he tends to lose control during rest time, it may help to let him play with a toy so that he doesn't easily drift into semi-sleep and "let go."

The guidelines here are to pay more attention to wetting and soiling in an older child, as they may be symptoms of psychological disturbance. The older the child and the more often it happens, the more likelihood there is of deep-seated problems. It is best to treat the temporary loss of control merely as a happening, like the loss of other kinds of control we all experience now and then. Some people lose sphincter control, and some people lose their temper. Once done, the results usually can be tidied up fairly quickly with no great embarrassment. Youngsters should be encouraged to look on their inner body mechanisms as highly efficient, and in this sense as beautiful as the outer body, and certainly nothing to be ashamed of. Although the body emissions are waste matter with a negative connotation, the process is positive and essential to the miraculous body mechanism.

If you believe that wetting or soiling in a youngster is a symptom of disturbance rather than an accidental loss of control, the first step is to try to arrange some professional psychological help for him.

4

The School's Community

This small chapter will end our small book. In it we want to share our thoughts about the optimal relationship of school and community. The minor themes have been sounded in earlier chapters but this is a summary attempt to share the colors, textures, rhythm, and warmth of schools as we experience them today and hope to experience them in the future.

SAVE OUR PLANET

We are all caught up in day-to-day concerns; a puzzling ailment for which we must seek medical attention, a bill that is overdue and must be paid, a friend who is troubled and needs some time and attention, a long-awaited vacation that now can be planned, weddings, births, funerals, birthdays, or haunting memories of important events in the past. They are the warp of human life; worked through by chance circumstances and intentional effort, they shape the fabric of our experience. But we forget sometimes to look up at the stars and feel the truth that we are minute beings on a small planet that is finding its own way through space.

There is a big question in front of us. It is so big that we seldom see it. The question is whether humans will survive on this planet. Will the great human experiment be a success? Or will we kill ourselves in wars or choke in our own waste products? Ecology is a more popular topic today but it is not only a field of study or a topic of conversation. We are chatting about our survival as a species. We are talking about the death of our children and grandchildren.

Humans are endlessly involved in disputes with one another. Some of the disputes are productive because they present alternatives that contribute to creative problem solving. But human children are the closest thing we have to an agreeable common denominator. Almost everyone is touched by a small child who is searching for solutions to problems as he reaches out in wonder to the world around him. Hardly any adult can resist offering a helping hand to a lost child. We want children to live. We want them to find their way.

There is a fact we must face. We are making our planet uninhabitable because of our ruthless war and waste. It must stop, or all of the other "causes," all of the other debates over right and wrong are empty. The battle being fought by blacks in our nation—and other forms of struggle for freedom from oppression—are terribly important. This struggle has the dignity of the human being at its heart. The struggle must continue to a successful end, but we had better keep perspective. The ecological battle must have priority. It must not displace the struggle for freedom, but when a choice is to be made, energy must go into the ecological struggle. Unless future life is possible on this planet there is no use in anything.

Because a child wants to live, he wants to learn. Anyone who has carefully observed an infant grow into childhood sees the relentless search for information about how to stay alive. Information is sought before the child can even speak and once he has words available there is an endless flow of questions. That child wants to stay alive. He wants to survive. And one of his assets is that he wants to live with other people and other animals. Unless he is damaged while growing, he seeks out the company of others. He will gladly take all of the help that is clearly relevant to his quest for survival.

We have created something called "school" to help him with his searching. We must face the fact that our concept of school is too often geared to helping a child solve problems that exist in the world of today or yesterday. The world has changed and it is going to keep changing at an increasingly faster pace. If schools are to make any sense they must help a child learn to solve problems that do not exist or do not make much sense in the world of today or yesterday. Impossible? It is quite possible if we adults with our liability of limited imagination do not get in the path of young creativity.

A child must learn new ways to live with his fellow humans, other animals, and other forms of life. He must learn new ways to approach problems. He must feel free to use his imagination and creativity to solve problems unimagined by his teachers. He must use school to learn how to stay alive and keep the planet fit for his children and their children. It is something we have not learned in our schools up to now.

Schools are our only real hope in saving our planet. Newspapers and books do not reach everyone. Television and movies do not reach everyone. Our schools are the only social units in which adults who represent the culture are in touch with all of our growing young. Most of us who work in the field of education have had private moments of despair about our schools, yet they are our only hope. If our schools cannot help the young learn something about survival, we must face the truth that they will not learn it. Survival is no longer a private matter. No individual can survive long in the coming century unless he has learned cooperative living with his fellow man. For better or worse, our schools must be used to save our planet and make it a place that is safe for children.

USE OUR SCHOOLS

A young friend recently moved, along with his intended wife, into a communal family of ten. In response to our questions, he explained that the family has rules for sharing expenses, food preparation, and house cleaning. But the rules are not strict. Each family member tries to remember that it is his pleasure to help the other family members live a richer life. We asked questions about feelings involved when one person pays more money or works longer hours or changes sex partners. Much of the family life runs counter to our culture's unspoken laws of acquisition and possession. After an hour of discussion it was clear to us that these people are trying to do something far more rational than following the habits of their grandparents. But our discomfort lingered.

Those of us who are over thirty, and many who are still under thirty, are frequently reminded that this is a new world. It is changing faster every day. We cannot do things the "good old way," whether we want to or not. Old habits must yield to new ideas.

A housewife who spends all of her working hours planning the best means of storing, preserving, and caring for her food supply instead of searching for the best ways to use it up is someone who needs perspective on her job. Yet as educators we are often in the same spot. The way we view the buildings that house our schools is a good example. We endlessly build new ones, seek to preserve old ones, and use both as little as possible so as to cut down on costs for repair and maintainance. That is foolish. We should be figuring out ways to use them up. We should be trying to wear them out.

We spend millions of dollars on a building that is used during 25 per cent of the hours that tick by in the calendar year. Imagine the uses that the building could have during the other hours if we were not so caught up in taking care of it. Imagine that the building were used as a genuine community center. With a little luck we might be able to use it 70 per cent of the time!

The building could become a center for medical services, entertainment, town meetings, instruction for people regardless of age, social services, festivals, fund-raising activities, memorial services, meditation, idea exchange forums, human potential exploration activities, or any other communal activity. Children might be able to make use of the building after dark. Grownups might be able to learn there or socialize there during daylight hours. Imagine what an exciting center for human community activity it could be! Instead of the dull daytime prison it too often is now, it could be a place of wonder and excitement—a meeting place.

There are many possible new approaches to school learning. Let the seven-year-old go to a learning situation with his thirteen-year-old sister, or with his father, or with the spinster lady neighbor who has all of those cats. Let anyone who is interested come for a beginning experience with conversational Japanese, or instruction in ceramic crafts, or advanced experimentation with new math. We pay lip service to the idea of adult and child learning together. How about having them go to school together? Why must we keep children of the same age together for a certain number of hours each day? There may be some advantage for chronological peers grouping together now and then but there is more obvious advantage in mixing age and experience in a situation where interest in learning about something is the uniting bond.

Of course, to take advantage of such new ideas (old ideas really if you think of the one-room schoolhouse), we may have to rethink our definitions of words like *respect* and *pride*. Many adults would feel uncomfortable sitting next to a five-year-old and learning a new language *with* him. But then adults have been fattened on myths about grownups knowing all the answers. Some adults have been deluded sufficiently to believe that they must pretend to know answers they do not know or youngsters will not have respect for them. It is obvious that the respect is as artificial as the foundation on which it rests, but some adults have not thought it through clearly enough to see that. New ways of doing things are frightening to adults. But old ways will not see us through to survival, and *that* is even more frightening.

Genuine efforts toward chronological integration might nip our generation-gap problems in the bud. There could hardly be a generation gap if seven-year-olds and seventy-year-olds were colleagues in learning. And imagine the fascinating stories that those old folks could tell interested young listeners. And imagine the lonely hours and empty laps those seven-year-olds could warm. We are wasting our human resources.

A school could be a corridor for the community. It could still have classrooms. The rooms could be filled with various people who want to learn about the same thing. A "course" could run for an hour or four years. It could run from seven in the morning to ten in the evening, or be offered six half hours a year. Each family could have its own locker in the school. All of this and much more could be if we would let it be. A school could belong to the people of a community, but fear holds us back.

FIGHTING FEAR AND HELPING ONE ANOTHER

Our schools reflect the suspicion and hostility prevalent in our contemporary world. People do not trust one another. Teachers do not trust parents, administrators do not trust teachers, parents do not trust school personnel in general. And all of this has some foundation in fact. As long as people continue to categorize one another and be self-protective, the suspicion and hostility will continue. It is time to begin to decategorize human beings. You are not just a teacher, you are a person.

Parents and teachers share adult interest in the welfare of the children who are now in school. No parent likes to feel that his children have been taken over by the school during school hours. It is uncomfortable for a parent to be called in by a teacher and told what is right and wrong with his son or daughter.

We can begin to break the vicious circle if we who are teachers also begin to think of ourselves as people who happen to have a service to offer. We can offer it in the most tempting ways possible to all interested customers. For the time being we can concentrate on tempting children and parents. We can listen to parents tell of their hopes and dreams for their children. We can listen to children tell of their daily concerns and their worries for the future. Then we can think about the wares that we are offering and think how they can best enrich the real lives of these people. In what way can this spelling or chemistry make sense to the needs of these parents and children in this neighborhood? Rather than expecting the customer to answer this question, those of us who are selling the product had better answer it if we are to tempt them to buy.

It is too easy for us as professional educators to think of schools as *our* establishment into which we permit children and parents to enter. A teacher easily speaks of "my classroom," a principal of "my school." We are permitted to work there, but the owners are the parents and children who make up the community we serve. They are our employers. If we live in the community it is *our* class-room, a place that shelters us from the elements while we try to learn. If we live outside of the community we enter as a hired con-sultant or specialist, a guest, and paid because the natives believe we have something to offer.

As teachers we must be alert not to shut out parents. Parents live with children around the clock for years. We teachers work with those children for some hours. Our work had better make sense within the context of the local world these children live in with their parents, or the usual child will reject what we have to offer as amusing or dull nonsense. Parents are necessary allies in selling educational products and we had better try to endear our-selves to those parents. Parents can be (and often are) bullied by teachers but anyone knows that a bully is not a good friend or ally. A bully is someone to cajole and then escape from as quickly as possible. So let us not delude ourselves into believing that a charm-ing smile can truly mask bullying behavior. You cannot make a parent do what you want him to do. You cannot force a parent to force a child to become an eager customer of your educational product. You can only force them to go through the motions until they can find a way to be free of you. You *can* alter your product, though, until it more clearly meets the needs of your customers. That is a part of the job of an educator.

There is an unresolved and partly unresolvable argument running as to whether it is better for teachers to come from within the community or from outside of the community. Chances are that both sides of the argument are right. Teachers who are genuinely a part of the community have a lot of information about their customers. They know what kind of food they eat, what they watch on television, how much privacy there usually is in the home, the values that show up in dreams, feuds, and purchasing, which behavior is considered fun, and which is considered indecent. A teacher from outside the community, with determined effort, can learn much of this, but may never have a feel of the *gestalt*. He may know what food is eaten but he does not have the subtle associations to each dish because he has not grown up with the smell of it cooking. Unless most teacher-training institutions mend their ways, it is unlikely that a teacher from outside the community will know much of anything about how it feels to live in the community. The official professional attitude for years has been to keep a safe, antiseptic distance from the child's home. Parents are called into the fortress of the school instead of letting teachers walk through the unsafe, foreign alley-ways of the community. But times are changing. In some areas teachers are making the once-a-year home visit that was respectable a few decades ago. This is a little better than nothing, but of course it hardly gives a feel of the community. You can get a feel of how each family goes about putting its best foot forward to entertain a visiting dignitary but you will remain an ignorant foreigner.

Yet if all of the teachers are from within the community how are the youngsters to stretch their horizons? They need the kind of understanding that home-grown teachers can offer, but most such teachers have the same subtle limitations as the children. It takes a "foreigner" to do things differently with sufficient grace and assurance to make the children question their own accustomed ways.

It is much the same thing that foreign travel to exotic places does to stretch the horizons of the affluent.

The answer here is probably that the children need to have the best of both worlds. They need plenty of friendly, understanding adults from the community around them and they need exposure to some foreigners who can shake them loose from complacency and stimulate them to think in new ways.

Can we work together? Can teachers, administrators, parents, children, community groups, and any other interested citizens get together for the welfare of the community? Of course it can be done. There is nothing stopping us but ourselves. Nothing is in our path except our own fear and suspicion. The teacher fears the prying parent who will charge incompetence and possibly cause him to lose his job. The parent fears the contemptuous teacher who will laugh at his simple, uneducated ways and make him ridiculous in the eyes of his children. The administrator fears a community takeover that will leave him without power to do what he believes best. Where it will all go is anyone's guess.

The struggle is now part of the current social revolution. We must ride the crest of this wave of revolution, and remember our goals, or we will drown. If you are an educator, you are interested in the survival of your students. While riding the crest of the wave it is well to remember that achieving your educational objectives may call for the sacrifice of false dignity, pride, and comfort. You may even get a few bruises, but if you land upright on the beach it will all have been worthwhile. If you can help to remake schools into social units that promote human survival and seek the dignity of each person, you will have spent your professional life well. For the sake of you and me and our children, perhaps we will work together in an atmosphere of sharing concern.

HUMAN COMMUNITIES

The class or the learning group is a temporary community. The school is a larger surrounding community. The neighborhood is still a larger surrounding community. The state and the nation are larger surrounding communities. Our planet is a larger surrounding community. We do not yet know what larger surrounding communities there are. But it is obvious that all else that is offered in school is of little or no use if the youngster does not learn to use it in the context of *community*.

We want to help the growing human retain his curiosity and his natural urges to acquire information and work toward the solution of problems and the resolution of conflict. Teachers are human and students are human. We have tried to point out how easy it is to lose perspective and get caught up in roles that deny the humanness we all have in common. We have also tried to point out how it is possible to step back a moment, regain perspective, smile or frown at one another, and seek human answers to human questions. We are working and living in groups—human groups. We are working and living as persons who want to grow into the unforseeable future—a human future. Good luck to us all!

BIBLIOGRAPHY

Adler, Alfred, *Social Interests: A Challenge to Mankind.* New York: G. P. Putnam's Sons, 1964.

Argyris, Chris, *Personality and Organization.* New York: Harper & Row, Publishers, 1957.

Alschuler, Alfred S., "Psychological Education," *Achievement Motivation Development Project, Working Paper No. 1.* Cambridge, Mass.: Harvard University Press, 1968.

Amidon, Edmund and Elizabeth Hunter, *Improving Teaching: The Analysis of Classroom Verbal Interaction.* New York: Holt, Rinehart & Winston, Inc., 1967.

Ashby, Gail, "The Child I Was," *This Magazine is About Schools,* III, 2 (1969), 25–381.

Ashton-Warner, Sylvia, *Teacher.* New York: Simon & Schuster, Inc., 1963.

Bakker, Piet, *Ciske the Rat.* London: Michael Joseph, 1958.

Borton, Terry, "Reach, Touch, Teach," *Saturday Review,* LII, 3 (1969), 56–70.

Borton, Terry, *Reach, Touch, and Teach.* New York: McGraw-Hill Book Company, 1970.

Borton, Terry, "What Turns Kids On," *Saturday Review,* L, 15 (1967), 72–74.

Baruch, Dorothy W., *One Little Boy.* New York: Julian Press, Inc., 1952.

Berlin, I. L., "From Teachers' Problems to Problem Teachers," *Mental Hygiene,* XLIV (1960), 80–83.

Berne, Eric, *Games People Play.* New York: Grove Press, Inc., 1964.

Bessell, Harold, "The Content Is The Medium: The Confidence Is The Message," *Psychology Today,* I, 8 (1968), 32–61.

Bettelheim, Bruno, *Dialogues with Mothers.* New York: The Free Press of Glencoe, The Macmillan Company, 1962.

Bettelheim, Bruno, *Love Is Not Enough.* New York: The Free Press of Glencoe, The Macmillan Company, 1950.

Bettelheim, Bruno, *Truants From Life.* New York: The Free Press of Glencoe, The Macmillan Company, 1955.

Bloom, Benjamin, Allison Davis, and Robert Hess, *Compensatory Education for Cultural Deprivation.* New York: Holt, Rinehart & Winston, Inc., 1965.

Braithwaite, E. R., *To Sir With Love.* Englewood Cliffs, N. J.: Prentice-Hall Inc., 1960.

Bronfenbrenner, U., "The Changing American Child—A Speculative Analysis," *Journal of Social Issues,* XVII (1961), 6–18.

Brown, Claude, *Manchild in the Promised Land.* New York: The Macmillan Company, 1965.

Brown, George I., *Human Teaching for Human Learning.* New York: McGraw-Hill Book Company, 1970.

Brown, George Isaac, "*Now: the Human Dimension*," Esalen Monograph No. 1. Big Sur, Calif.: Esalen Institute, 1968.

Bruner, Jerome S., *The Process of Education.* Cambridge, Mass.: Harvard University Press, 1966.

Bugental, James F. T., *Challenges of Humanistic Psychology.* New York: McGraw-Hill Book Co., 1967.

Buhler, Charlotte, *Childhood Problems and the Teacher.* New York: Holt, Rinehart & Winston, Inc., 1952.

Burns, Robert C., and S. Harvard Kaufman, *Kinetic Family Drawings (K-F-D).* New York: Brunner/Mazel, Inc., 1970.

Chase, Virginia, *The End of the Week.* The Macmillan Company, 1953.

Children of Poverty—Children of Affluence. New York: The Child Study Association of America, Inc., 1967.

Clark, Donald H., Arlene Goldsmith, and Clementine Pugh, *Those Children.* Belmont, Calif.: Wadsworth Publishing Co., 1970.

Clark, Donald H. and Gerold S. Lesser, *Emotional Disturbance and School Learning.* Chicago: Science Research Associates, 1965.

Corsini, Raymond J. and Daniel D. Howard, *Critical Incidents in Teaching.* Englewood Cliffs, N. J.: Prentice-Hall Inc., 1964.

D'Amico, Victor, *Experiments in Creative Art Teaching.* New York: The Museum of Modern Art, 1960.

Davis, David C. L., *Model for a Humanistic Education: The Danish Folk Highschool.* Columbus, Ohio: Charles E. Merrill Publishing Company, 1971.

deMille, Richard, *Put Your Mother on the Ceiling.* New York: Walker & Company, 1967.

Division of School Psychology, "The School Psychologist," American Psychological Association, 1970.

Donovan, Frank, *Raising Your Child.* Chicago: Cromwell Textbooks, Inc., 1968.

Erickson, E. H., *Childhood and Society.* New York: W. W. Norton & Co., 1945.

Esty, G. "*The Child Who is Dirty and Smells Bad,*" *The Instructor,* LXXI (1964), 46–47.

Fagan, Joen, and Irma Lee Shepard (eds.), *Gestalt Therapy Now: Theory, Techniques, Applications.* Palo Alto, Calif.: Science and Behavior Books, Inc., 1970.

Fantini, Mario D. and Gerald Weinstein, "Taking Advantage of the Disadvantaged," *The Record,* Teachers' College, Columbia University, LXII, 2 (1967), 2–12.

Fifty Teachers to a Classroom, Committee on Human Resources, Metropolitan School Study Council. New York: The Macmillan Company, 1950.

Fraiberg, Selma H., *The Magic Years.* New York: Charles Scribners' Sons, 1959.

Friedenberg, Edgar, *Coming of Age in America.* New York: Random House, Inc., 1965.

Friedenberg, Edgar, *The Vanishing Adolescent.* New York: Dell Publishing Co., Inc., 1962.

Frost, J. L. (ed.), *Early Childhood Education Rediscovery.* New York: Holt, Rinehart & Winston, Inc., 1969.

Gardner, D. E. M. and J. E. Cass, *The Role of the Teacher in the Infant and Nursery School.* New York: Pergamon Press, Inc., 1965.

Georgine, Constantine, *Children and Their Literature.* Englewood Cliffs, N. J: Prentice-Hall, Inc., 1968.

Gideonse, Hendrik D., "Projecting Alternative Futures: Implications for Educational Goals, Achievements and Challenges," The New Forum Papers, 2nd Series. Washington, D. C.: U. S. Department of Health, Education, and Welfare, 1968–1969.

Goodman, Paul, *Growing Up Absurd.* New York: Vintage Books, Inc., 1962.

Green, Maxine, *Existential Encounters for Teachers.* New York: Random House, Inc., 1967.

Grossman, L. and D. Clark, "Sensitivity Training for Teachers: a Small Group Approach," *Psychology in the Schools,* IV (1967), 267–271.

Hall, Mary Harrington, "A Conversation With Carl Rogers," *Psychology Today,* I, 7 (1967), 19–69.

Helping Teachers to Understand Children, Washington, D. C.: American Council on Education, 1948.

Hentoff, Nat, *Our Children Are Dying.* New York: The Viking Press, 1967.

Herndon, James, *The Way It Spozed to Be.* New York: Simon & Schuster, Inc., 1968.

Holt, John, *How Children Fail.* New York: Pitman Publishing Corp., 1964.

Holt, John. *How Children Learn.* New York: Pitman Publishing Corp., 1967.

Hunter, E. C., "Changes in Teachers' Attitudes Toward Children's Behavior Over the Last Thirty Years," *Mental Hygiene*, XLI (1957), 3–11.

Huxley, A., "Education on the Non-Verbal Level," *Daedalus*, Cambridge, Mass: American Association for the Advancement of Science, Spring 1962.

James, Deborah, *The Taming*. New York: McGraw-Hill Book Co., Inc., 1969.

Jersild, Arthur T.,*When Teachers Face Themselves*. New York: Columbia University Press, 1955.

Jones, Richard M.,*Fantasy and Feeling in Education*. New York: New York University Press; London: University of London Press Ltd., 1968.

Jordan, June, *Who Look at Me*. New York: Thomas Y. Crowell Co., 1969.

Joseph, Stephen M. (ed.), *The Me Nobody Knows: Children's Voices From the Ghetto*. New York: Avon Books, 1969.

The Journal of Social Issues, XV, 1 (1959). Entire issue devoted to Mental Health in the Classroom.

Kadis, Asya L., Jack D. Krasner, Charles Winick, and S. H. Foulkes, *A Practicum of Group Psychotherapy*. New York: Harper & Row, Publishers, 1963.

Kadis, A. L., C. Winick, and E. Clark, "The Teachers' Educational Process Workshop," *The Record*, Teachers College, Columbia University Press, IV (1969), 297–311.

Kaufman, Belle, *Up The Down Staircase*. New York: Avon Books, 1966.

Kellogg, Rhoda, and Scott O'Dell, *The Psychology of Children's Art*. Random House, Inc., 1967.

Kohl, Herbert, *36 Children*. New York: New American Library, 1967.

Konopka, Gisela, *Therapeutic Group Work With Children*. Minneapolis: University of Minnesota Press; London: Geoffrey Cumberlege, Oxford University Press, 1949.

Kozol, Jonathan, *Death at an Early Age*. Boston: Houghton Mifflin Company, 1967.

Laing, R. D., *The Politics of Experience*. New York: Pantheon Books, Inc., Random House, Inc., 1967.

Lederman, Janet, *Anger and the Rocking Chair*. New York: McGraw-Hill Book Co., 1969.

Leonard, George B., *Education and Ecstasy*. New York: Delacorte Press, 1968.

Levitt, Helen, *A Way of Seeing*. New York: The Viking Press, 1965.

Lewis, Oscar, *La Vida*. New York: Random House, Inc., 1965.

Lifton, Walter M., *Working with Groups: Group Process and Individual Growth*. New York: John Wiley & Sons, Inc., 1961.

Lindgren, Henry Clay, *Educational Psychology in the Classroom* (3rd ed.). New York: John Wiley & Sons, Inc., 1967.

Lyon, Harold C., Jr. *Learning to Feel—Feeling to Learn: Humanistic Education for the Whole Man*. Columbus, Ohio: Charles E. Merrill Publishing Company, 1971.

Malamud, Daniel I. and Solomon Machover, *Toward Self Understanding*. Springfield, Ill.: Charles C. Thomas, 1965.

Mallery, David, *New Approaches in Education: A Study of Experimental Programs in Independent Schools*. Boston: National Council of Independent Schools, 1961.

Marsh, L., *Alongside the Child: Experiences in the English Primary School*. New York: Frederick A. Praeger, Inc., 1970.

Maslow, Abraham, *Goals of Humanistic Education*. Big Sur, Calif.: Esalen Institute, 1968.

McKean, William J., "Encounter: How Kids Turn Off Drugs," *Look*, April 15, 1969, 40–42.

Miles, Matthew B., *Learning to Work in Groups*. New York: Teachers' College Press, Columbia University, 1959.

Millar, S., *The Psychology of Play*. New York: Penguin Books, Inc., 1969.

Moreno, J. L. (ed.), *The International Handbook of Group Psychotherapy*. New York: Philosophical Library, Inc., 1966.

Naranjo, Claudio, *The Unfolding of Man*, Research Memorandum No. 6747-3, Menlo Park, Calif.: Educational Policy Research Center, Stanford Research Institute, 1969.

Otto, Herbert A. and John Mann, *Ways of Growth: Approaches to Expanding Awareness*. New York: Grossman Publishers, Inc., 1968.

Peel, E. A., *The Psychological Basis of Education*. Edinburgh, Scotland: Oliva & Boyd, 1958.

Perceiving, Behaving, Becoming, Yearbook Committee of the Association for Supervision and Curriculum Development, National Education Association, 1962.

Perls, Frederick, *Gestalt Therapy Verbatim*. Lafayette, Calif.: Real People Press, 1969.

Pitcher, Evelyn Goodenough and Ernst Prelinger, *Children Tell Stories: An Analysis of Fantasy*. New York: International Universities Press, Inc., 1963.

Redl, Fritz and W. Wattenberg, *Mental Hygiene in Teaching*. New York: Harcourt, Brace & World, Inc., 1959.

Redl, Fritz, *When We Deal With Children*. New York: The Free Press of Glencoe,The Macmillan Company, 1966.

Reisman, Frank, *The Culturally Deprived Child*. New York: Harper & Row, Publishers, 1963.

Rogers, Carl R., "The Characteristics of a Helping Relationship," *The Personnel and Guidance Journal*, XXXVII (1958), 6–16.

Rogers, Carl R., *Freedom to Learn*. Columbus, Ohio: Charles E. Merrill Publishing Company, 1969.

Rogers, Carl R., "The Group Comes of Age," *Psychology Today*, III (1969), 27–61.

Rosenthal, R. and L. Jacobson, *Pygmalion in the Classroom*. New York: Holt, Rinehart & Winston, Inc., 1968.

Sarason, S. B., F. F. Lighthall, K. S. Davidson, R. R. Waite, and B. K. Rue-bush, *Anxiety in Elementary School Children.* New York: John Wiley & Sons, Inc., 1960.

Schlesinger, Roger, "The French on Life and Love," Edward Lewis (ed.). Hallmark Cards, Inc., 1967.

Schoenfeld, Eugene, *Dear Doctor Hippocrates.* New York: Grove Press, 1968.

Schwitzgebel, Robert L., *Streetcorner Research.* Cambridge, Mass.: Harvard University Press, 1964.

Sexton, Patricia Cayo, *Spanish Harlem: Anatomy of Poverty.* New York: Harper & Row, Publishers, 1965.

Shepard, Martin and Marjorie Lee, *Games Analysts Play.* New York: G. P. Putnam's Sons, 1970.

Silberman, Charles E., *Crisis in the Classroom.* New York: Random House, Inc., 1970.

Simon, D. and D. Sarkotich, "Sensitivity Training in the Classroom," *National Education Association Journal,* LVI, 1 (January 1967), 12–13.

Spark, Muriel, *The Prime of Miss Jean Brodie.* Philadelphia: J. B. Lippincott Co., 1961.

Stein, Maurice R., Arthur J. Vidich, and David Manning White, *Identity and Anxiety.* New York: The Free Press of Glencoe, The Macmillan Company, 1960.

Sutich, Anthony J. and Miles A. Vitch, *Readings in Humanistic Psychology.* New York: The Free Press of Glencoe, The Macmillan Company, 1969.

Taba, H. and D. Elkind, *Teaching Strategies for the Culturally Disadvantaged.* New York: Rand McNally & Co., 1966.

Valentine, C. W., *The Normal Child and Some of His Abnormalities.* Baltimore: Penguin Books, Inc., 1956.

Winnicott, D. W., *The Child, the Family, and the Outside World.* Baltimore: Penguin Books, Inc., 1964.

Wittenberg, Rudolph M., *Adolescence and Discipline.* New York: Association Press, 1959.

Wolff, Werner, *The Personality of the Pre-School Child.* New York: Grune & Stratton, Inc., 1947.

Wright, Betty Atwell, "Helping Children Understand Why They Feel as They Do," *National Education Association Journal,* XLVIII (1960), 24.

INDEX